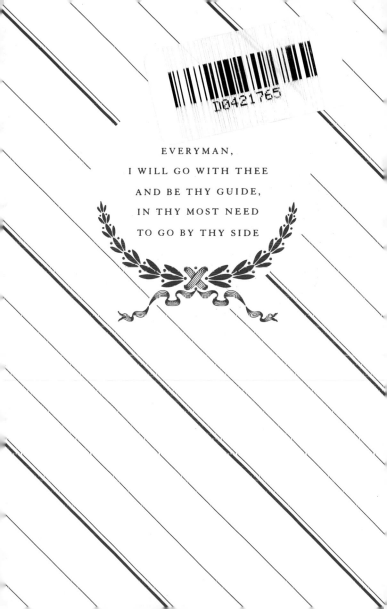

EVERYMAN,
I WILL GO WITH THEE
AND BE THY GUIDE,
IN THY MOST NEED
TO GO BY THY SIDE

EVERYMAN'S LIBRARY
POCKET POETS

POEMS
ABOUT
HORSES

••••••••••••••••••••

EDITED BY
CARMELA CIURARU

EVERYMAN'S LIBRARY
POCKET POETS

Alfred A. Knopf New York London Toronto

THIS IS A BORZOI BOOK
PUBLISHED BY ALFRED A. KNOPF

This selection by Carmela Ciuraru first published in
Everyman's Library, 2009
Copyright © 2009 by Everyman's Library

A list of acknowledgments to copyright owners appears at the back
of this volume.

US website: www.randomhouse.com/everymans

ISBN 978-0-307-26925-6 (US)
978-1-84159-784-3 (UK)

A CIP catalogue record for this book is available from the British Library

Typography by Peter B. Willberg
Typeset in the UK by AccComputing, North Barrow, Somerset
Printed and bound in Germany by GGP Media GmbH, Pössneck

CONTENTS

ON THE FARM, OFF TO THE HUNT

WAR HORSES

8

CELEBRATION AND REMEMBRANCE

FOREWORD

Icons of power, speed, and civilization since they were first domesticated thousands of years ago, horses are among the most majestic creatures to wander the earth. The extent to which humans' lives have been enriched by these animals is immeasurable: many of our most basic habits of work, play, transport, and warfare would have been impossible without them. It is no wonder that this profound relationship has inspired countless works of art, from ancient times to the present. This collection is a sampling across the centuries of the ways horses have been contemplated and celebrated in poetry.

The horse has served as warrior, laborer, mail carrier, competitive athlete, rodeo entertainer, friend, and – above all – object of wonder. In this anthology's opening section, 'Entering the World', Ted Hughes offers a tender evocation of a foal's first steps on the way to becoming 'perfect Horse': 'His nose / Downy and magnetic, draws him, incredulous, / Towards his mother. And the world is warm / And careful and gentle. Touch by touch / Everything fits him together.'

The following section, 'Horse and Rider', focuses on the elemental human–horse connection, with poems by E. E. Cummings, Basil Bunting, and Richard Wilbur, along with perhaps the most famous contemporary poem about a journey on horseback — Robert Frost's

'Stopping by Woods on a Snowy Evening' – in which a horse, for a change, wonders at human mystery.

'Horses in Mind' ventures into abstract and dreamlike manifestations. For Witter Bynner and Sylvia Plath, untamed horses are apt metaphors for the elusiveness of language. Paul Muldoon ponders 'if I'm a man dreaming I'm a plowhorse / or a great plowhorse dreaming I'm a man.' And Carl Phillips imagines that a 'horse is entering / the sea, and the sea / holds it.'

Elsewhere, horses are honored for their pastoral and hunting work by poets such as Gary Snyder, Maxine Kumin, and Seamus Heaney. Poems by Homer, Virgil, Shakespeare, Tennyson, and others commemorate the horse's role in battle, and a brief section touches on the colorful tradition of cowboy poetry on the American frontier.

The poems in 'Equine Encounters' describe revelatory meetings between our species, and in the final section poets honor the horse in memory and in grief. 'They have pulled our ploughs and borne our load,' writes Edwin Muir. 'But that free servitude still can pierce our hearts.' Thanks to the amazing bond we have known with horses throughout history, 'Our life is changed; their coming our beginning.'

CARMELA CIURARU

ENTERING THE WORLD

From WHAT IS THE TRUTH?

'New Foal'

Yesterday he was nowhere to be found
In the skies or under the skies.

Suddenly he's here – a warm heap
Of ashes and embers, fondled by small draughts.

A star dived from outer space – flared
And burned out in the straw.
Now something is stirring in the smoulder.
We call it a foal.

Still stunned
He has no idea where he is.
His eyes, dew-dusky, explore gloom walls and a glare
    doorspace.
Is this the world?
It puzzles him. It is a great numbness.

He pulls himself together, getting used to the weight
    of things
And to that tall horse nudging him, and to this straw.

He rests
From the first blank shock of light, the empty daze
Of the questions –
What has happened? What am I?

His ears keep on asking, gingerly.

But his legs are impatient,
Recovering from so long being nothing
They are restless with ideas, they start to try
    a few out,
Angling this way and that,
Feeling for leverage, learning fast –

And suddenly he's up

And stretching – a giant hand
Strokes him from nose to heel
Perfecting his outline, as he tightens
The knot of himself.
                Now he comes teetering
Over the weird earth. His nose
Downy and magnetic, draws him, incredulous,
Towards his mother. And the world is warm
And careful and gentle. Touch by touch
Everything fits him together.

Soon he'll be almost a horse.
He wants only to be Horse,
Pretending each day more and more Horse
Till he's perfect Horse. Then unearthly Horse
Will surge through him, weightless, a spinning
      of flame
Under sudden gusts,

It will coil his eyeball and his heel
In a single terror – like the awe
Between lightning and thunderclap.

And curve his neck, like a sea-monster emerging
Among foam,

And fling the new moons through his stormy banner,
And the full moons and the dark moons.

PULLING INTO MORNING

As if a river twisting back upon itself,
The foal arrived as the mare died. One breath ends
At the start of another; one more way

Into the world. The sun rose, the song
Of the rooster broke over the barn,
And I kept at my notebook with any odd detail

Of labor, of transition. I carefully wrote
Until it became an old horse, an awkward colt
And a bad night. She may or may not have known
What she was carrying. She may or may not

Have heard your hooves hit ground.
Even in the earnest light of your rising, you will
    never know
How you came to be. You lean into my arms
Until I no longer feel them. There is no rest.

BRUTE MYSTIC

A Foal had been born,
had emerged on thin stilts
from the tobacco barn,
and with woodchips stuck
to it. An ice cream truck
looked lost and dragged
behind it a string of soup
and corn cans. I sat
on the porch and forced
my thoughts onto the lawn.
Very pale-looking, sure.
Very tightly gripping my beer can.
You sat with me.
You tipped back your head
so I could look down your throat.
The foal tottered by.
This is very awkward, you said.
Yes, I said.
This is, you said ... well ...
and then you nodded off.
Yes, I said.
And then I nodded off.

When I awoke you were gone.
And a faint rumbling from

the toolshed? All day
things had seemed a long way
off, as they sometimes do
to a man under chloroform.
A yellow bird flickered past
and I could hear the duck chasing
the cows around. I went
and stood on the lawn and
smoked cigarettes, one
after another. The sky was blue
and the grass was green.
I considered this
and blew a smoke-ring at
the cat, feeling suddenly
combustible, some dreamish,
autobiographical thoughts
floating past me tied to a raft.
And then I guess I nodded off.

When I awoke I was lying on the lawn,
my cigarette still burning
between my lips. I finished it
and stood up and flicked
the butt at a fencepost and walked
toward the barn. It's raining, I said
to myself and it was.
And I have to go feed the matted ones.

MICHAEL EARL CRAIG

BIRTH OF THE FOAL

As May was opening the rosebuds,
elder and lilac beginning to bloom,
it was time for the mare to foal.
She'd rest herself, or hobble lazily

after the boy who sang as he led her
to pasture, wading through the meadowflowers.
They wandered back at dusk, bone-tired,
the moon perched on a blue shoulder of sky.

Then the mare lay down,
sweating and trembling, on her straw in the stable.
The drowsy, heavy-bellied cows
surrounded her, waiting, watching, snuffing.

Later, when even the hay slept
and the shaft of the Plough pointed south,
the foal was born Hours the mare
spent licking the foal with its glue-blind eyes.

And the foal slept at her side,
a heap of feathers ripped from a bed.
Straw never spread as soft as this.
Milk or snow never slept like a foal.

Dawn bounced up in a bright red hat,
waved at the world and skipped away.
Up staggered the foal,
its hooves were jelly-knots of foam.

Then day sniffed with its blue nose
through the open stable window, and found them –
the foal nuzzling its mother,
velvet fumbling for her milk.

Then all the trees were talking at once,
chickens scrabbled in the yard,
like golden flowers
envy withered the last stars.

22   FERENC JUHÁSZ
     TRANS. DAVID WEVILL

MARE AND NEWBORN FOAL

When you die
there are bales of hay
heaped high in space
mean while
with my tongue
I draw the black straw
out of you
mean while
with your tongue
you draw the black straw out of me.

HORSE AND RIDER

BUFFALO BILL 'S

Buffalo Bill 's
defunct
        who used to
        ride a watersmooth-silver
                      stallion
and break onetwothreefourfive pigeonsjustlikethat
                                   Jesus

he was a handsome man
                    and what i want to know is
how do you like your blueeyed boy
Mister Death

THE RESCUE

The man sits in a timelessness
with the horse under him in time
to a movement of legs and hooves
upon a timeless sand.

Distance comes in from the foreground
present in the picture as time
he reads outward from
and comes from that beginning.

A wind blows in
and out and all about the man
as the horse ran
and runs to come in time.

A house is burning in the sand.
A man and horse are burning.
The wind is burning.
They are running to arrive.

STOPPING BY WOODS ON A
SNOWY EVENING

Whose woods these are I think I know,
His house is in the village though;
He will not see me stopping here
To watch his woods fill up with snow.

My little horse must think it queer
To stop without a farmhouse near
Between the woods and frozen lake
The darkest evening of the year.

He gives his harness bells a shake
To ask if there is some mistake.
The only other sound's the sweep
Of easy wind and downy flake.

The woods are lovely, dark and deep,
But I have promises to keep,
And miles to go before I sleep,
And miles to go before I sleep.

ROBERT FROST   29

THE FOUR HORSEMEN

In our country the hills lie like tawny lions
green in spring, turning yellow with summer
here and there oak trees, with cattle under them
and in the broadest valleys, villages.

If strangers come along, we notice them.
Like those four, resting their horses
by the small stream there, under the oak tree.

Riders, and even from the distance
I can tell their horses are splendid, well-fed
faster than ours, and their trappings expensive.

Even from here they seem unusual travelers.
There's the one with the sorrel, a heavy man
black-bearded, restless, he aims his gun
at every bird, as if eager for hunting.

The thin one can't stand still either.
He is picking the stalks that grow around him
stripping the oats off, twisting the hollow stems
into knots and whistles. His horse is the black stallion.

And the plump palomino, stomping to be off
belongs to the man in the pale overcoat
who remains stock still, as if content where they are.

The fourth, in the yellow Stetson, waits apart from
    the others.
Whether he is their friend or enemy is hard to say.
Have they come for a duel in this deserted pasture?

I would go close if I dared, either to welcome them
to the village or find out their business.
But there is something so strange in their manner –

the oats falling back in a circle around them, the ground
growing dark, a cloud breaking the sun's warmth.
Better go back to town and see what's doing.

Those four may mean no harm, but no good certainly.
And I keep thinking of the balance of things
and how we might change should they settle among us.

UPON THE HORSE AND HIS RIDER

There's one rides very sagely on the road,
Showing that he affects the gravest mode.
Another rides tantivy, or full trot,
To show much gravity he matters not.
Lo, here comes one amain, he rides full speed,
Hedge, ditch, nor miry bog, he doth not heed.
One claws it up-hill without stop or check,
Another down as if he'd break his neck.
Now every horse has his especial guider;
Then by his going you may know the rider.

Comparison.

Now let us turn our horse into a man,
His rider to a spirit, if we can.
Then let us, by the methods of the guider,
Tell every horse how he should know his rider.
Some go, as men, direct in a right way,
Nor are they suffered to go astray;
As with a bridle they are governed,
And kept from paths which lead unto the dead.
Now this good man has his especial guider,
Then by his going let him know his rider.
Some go as if they did not greatly care,
Whether of heaven or hell they should be heir.

The rein, it seems, is laid upon their neck,
They seem to go their way without a check.
Now this man too has his especial guider,
And by his going he may know his rider.
Some again run as if resolved to die,
Body and soul, to all eternity.
Good counsel they by no means can abide;
They'll have their course whatever them betide.
Now these poor men have their especial guider,
Were they not fools they soon might know their rider.
There's one makes head against all godliness,
Those too, that do profess it, he'll distress;
He'll taunt and flout if goodness doth appear,
And at its countenancers mock and jeer.
Now this man, too, has his especial guider,
And by his going he might know his rider.

'RIDE A COCKHORSE TO BANBURY CROSS'

Ride a cockhorse to Banbury Cross,
To see a fine lady upon a white horse;
Rings on her fingers and bells on her toes,
She shall have music wherever she goes.

THANKSGIVING DAY

Over the river and through the wood,
  To grandfather's house we go;
    The horse knows the way
    To carry the sleigh
  Through the white and drifted snow.

Over the river and through the wood —
  Oh, how the wind does blow!
    It stings the toes
    And bites the nose,
  As over the ground we go.

Over the river and through the wood,
  To have first-rate play.
    Hear the bells ring,
    'Ting-a-ling-ding!'
  Hurrah for Thanksgiving Day!

Over the river and through the wood,
  And straight through the barn-yard gate.
    We seem to go
    Extremely slow —
  It is so hard to wait!

Over the river and through the wood —
   Now grandmother's cap I spy!
      Hurrah for the fun!
      Is the pudding done?
   Hurrah for the pumpkin-pie!

SONNET XLI: HAVING THIS DAY MY HORSE

Having this day my horse, my hand, my lance
Guided so well that I obtain'd the prize,
Both by the judgment of the English eyes
And of some sent from that sweet enemy France;
Horsemen my skill in horsemanship advance,
Town folks my strength; a daintier judge applies
His praise to sleight which from good use doth rise;
Some lucky wits impute it but to chance;
Others, because of both sides I do take
My blood from them who did excel in this,
Think Nature me a man of arms did make.
How far they shot awry! The true cause is,
Stella look'd on, and from her heav'nly face
Sent forth the beams which made so fair my race.

ASTROPHEL AND STELLA XLIX

I on my horse, and Love on me, doth try
Our horsemanships, while by strange work I prove
A horseman to my horse, a horse to Love,
And now man's wrongs in me, poor beast, descry.
The reins wherewith my rider doth me tie
Are humbled thoughts, which bit of reverence move,
Curbed in with fear, but with gilt boss above
Of hope, which makes it seem fair to the eye.
The wand is will; thou, fancy, saddle art,
Girt fast by memory; and while I spur
My horse, he spurs with sharp desire to my heart;
He sits me fast, however I do stir;
And now hath made me to his hand so right
That in the manage myself takes delight.

HORSE

What does the horse give you
that I cannot give you?

I watch you when you are alone,
when you ride into the field behind the dairy,
your hands buried in the mare's
dark mane.

Then I know what lies behind your silence:
scorn, hatred of me, of marriage. Still,
you want me to touch you; you cry out
as brides cry, but when I look at you I see
there are no children in your body.
Then what is there?

Nothing, I think. Only haste
to die before I die.

In a dream, I watched you ride the horse
over the dry fields and then
dismount: you two walked together;
in the dark, you had no shadows.
But I felt them coming toward me
since at night they go anywhere,
they are their own masters.

Look at me. You think I don't understand?
What is the animal
if not passage out of this life?

THE RIDE

The horse beneath me seemed
To know what course to steer
Through the horror of snow I dreamed,
And so I had no fear,

Nor was I chilled to death
By the wind's white shudders, thanks
To the veils of his patient breath
And the mist of sweat from his flanks.

It seemed that all night through,
Within my hand no rein
And nothing in my view
But the pillar of his mane,

I rode with magic ease
At a quick, unstumbling trot
Through shattering vacancies
On into what was not,

Till the weave of the storm grew thin,
With a threading of cedar-smoke,
And the ice-blind pane of an inn
Shimmered, and I awoke.

How shall I now get back
To the inn-yard where he stands,
Burdened with every lack,
And waken the stable-hands

To give him, before I think
That there was no horse at all,
Some hay, some water to drink,
A blanket and a stall?

THE HORSE

. . . the glory of his nostrils is terrible.
                    Job 39:20

He kicked the world, and lunging long ago
Rose dripping with the dew of lawns,
Where new wind tapped him to a frieze
Against a wall of rising autumn leaves.
Some young foolhardy dweller of the barrows,
To grip his knees around the flanks,
Leaped from a tree and shivered in the air.
Joy clawed inside the bones
And flesh of the rider at the mane
Flopping and bounding over the dark banks.

Joy and terror floated on either side
Of the rider rearing. The supreme speed
Jerked to a height so spaced and wide
He seemed among the areas of the dead.
The flesh was free, the sky was rockless, clear,
The road beneath the feet was pure, the soul
Spun naked to the air
And lanced against a solitary pole
Of cumulus, to curve and roll
With the heave that disdains
Death in the body, stupor in the brains.

Now we have coddled the gods away.
The cool earth, the soft earth, we say:
Cover our eyes with petals, let the sky
Drift on while we are watching water pass
Among the drowsing mass
Of red and yellow algae in green lanes.
Yet earth contains
The horse as a remembrancer of wild
Arenas we avoid.

One day a stallion whirled my riding wife,
Whose saddle rocked her as a cradled child,
Gentle to the swell of water; yet her life
Poised perilously as on a shattered skiff.
The fear she rode, reminded of the void
That flung the ancient rider to the cold,
Dropped her down. I tossed my reins,

I ran to her with breath to make her rise,
And brought her back. Across my arms
She fumbled for the sunlight with her eyes.
I knew that she would never rest again,
For the colts of the dusk rear back their hooves
And paw us down, the mares of the dawn stampede
Across the cobbled hills till the lights are dead.
Here it is not enough to pray that loves
Draw grass over our childhood's lake of slime.

Run to the rocks where horses cannot climb,
Stable the daemon back to shaken earth,
Warm your hands at the comfortable fire,
Cough in a dish beside a wrinkled bed.

RIDING A NERVOUS HORSE

A dozen false starts:
You're such a fool, I said,
Spooking at shadows when
All day you were calm,
Placidly nosing the bushes
That now you pretend are strange,
Are struck with menace.

But he shuddered, stubborn
In his horsy posture,
Saying that I brought
Devils with me that he
Could hear gathering in all
The places behind him as I
Diverted his coherence
With my chatter and tack.

Indeed I have stolen
Something, a careful attention
I claim for my own yearning
Purpose, while he
Is left alone to guard
Us both from horse eaters
That merely grin at me
But I lust for him, for

The beauty of the haunch
My brush has polished, revealing
Treasures of edible light
In the shift of hide and hooves.

From VENUS AND ADONIS

Now which way shall she turn? What shall she say?
Her words are done, her woes the more increasing;
The time is spent, her object will away,
And from her twining arms doth urge releasing.
  'Pity,' she cries, 'some favour, some remorse!'
  Away he springs, and hasteth to his horse.

But lo, from forth a copse that neighbours by,
A breeding jennet, lusty, young and proud,
Adonis' trampling courser doth espy,
And forth she rushes, snorts and neighs aloud.
  The strong-necked steed, being tied unto a tree,
  Breaketh his rein and to her straight goes he.

Imperiously he leaps, he neighs, he bounds,
And now his woven girths he breaks asunder;
The bearing earth with his hard hoof he wounds,
Whose hollow womb resounds like heaven's thunder;
  The iron bit he crusheth 'tween his teeth,
  Controlling what he was controllèd with.

His ears up-pricked, his braided hanging mane
Upon his compassed crest now stand on end;
His nostrils drink the air, and forth again,
As from a furnace, vapours doth he send;

48

His eye, which scornfully glisters like fire,
Shows his hot courage and his high desire.

Sometime he trots, as if he told the steps,
With gentle majesty and modest pride;
Anon he rears upright, curvets and leaps,
As who should say, 'Lo, thus my strength is tried,
　　And this I do to captivate the eye
　　Of the fair breeder that is standing by.'

What recketh he his rider's angry stir,
His flattering 'Holla' or his 'Stand, I say'?
What cares he now for curb or pricking spur,
For rich caparisons or trappings gay?
　　He sees his love, and nothing else he sees,
　　For nothing else with his proud sight agrees.

Look when a painter would surpass the life
In limning out a well-proportioned steed,
His art with nature's workmanship at strife,
As if the dead the living should exceed;
　　So did this horse excel a common one
　　In shape, in courage, colour, pace and bone.

Round-hoofed, short-jointed, fetlocks shag and long,
Broad breast, full eye, small head and nostril wide,
High crest, short ears, straight legs and passing strong,
Thin mane, thick tail, broad buttock, tender hide;
    Look what a horse should have he did not lack,
    Save a proud rider on so proud a back.

Sometime he scuds far off, and there he stares;
Anon he starts at stirring of a feather;
To bid the wind a base he now prepares,
And where he run or fly they know not whether;
    For through his mane and tail the high wind sings,
    Fanning the hairs, who wave like feathered wings.

He looks upon his love and neighs unto her;
She answers him as if she knew his mind;
Being proud, as females are, to see him woo her,
She puts on outward strangeness, seems unkind,
    Spurns at his love and scorns the heat he feels,
    Beating his kind embracements with her heels.

'THAT FILLY COULDNT CARRY A RIDER'

That filly couldnt carry a rider nor
pull her weight in a plow team. How
could she stand up under a stallion?
All she thinks about is fields or a
brook when it's warm to plodge in.
Prancing round with the colts is her fun. Why
bite green apples? Come October they'll redden.
Then she'll match you: Time will give her the years
it snatches from you. She'll toss her head soon
to challenge a man, the besom, cuter
than Jane who hides or Leslie who lets her blouse
slip from her shining shoulder or even Jimmy.
You cant tell him from a girl if he keeps his mouth shut
with his long, loose hair and unguessable face.

(Horace)

YANKEE DOODLE

Yankee Doodle went to town,
A-riding on a pony;
Stuck a feather in his hat
And called it macaroni.

Yankee Doodle, keep it up
Yankee Doodle dandy,
Mind the music and the step
And with the girls be handy.

Father and I went down to camp
Along with Captain Gooding,
And there we saw the men and boys
As thick as hasty pudding.

Yankee Doodle, keep it up
Yankee Doodle dandy,
Mind the music and the step
And with the girls be handy.

There was Captain Washington
Upon a slapping stallion,
A-giving orders to his men;
I guess there were a million.

HORSES IN MIND

HORSES

Words are hoops
Through which to leap upon meanings,
Which are horses' backs,
Bare, moving.

WORDS

Axes
After whose stroke the wood rings,
And the echoes!
Echoes traveling
Off from the center like horses.

The sap
Wells like tears, like the
Water striving
To re-establish its mirror
Over the rock

That drops and turns,
A white skull,
Eaten by weedy greens.
Years later I
Encounter them on the road –

Words dry and riderless,
The indefatigable hoof-taps.
While
From the bottom of the pool, fixed stars
Govern a life.

A DREAM OF HORSES

We were born grooms, in stable-straw we sleep still,
All our wealth horse-dung and the combings of horses,
And all we can talk about is what horses ail.

Out of the night that gulfed beyond the palace-gate
There shook hooves and hooves and hooves of horses:
Our horses battered their stalls; their eyes jerked white.

And we ran out, mice in our pockets and straw
        in our hair,
Into darkness that was avalanching to horses
And a quake of hooves. Our lantern's little orange flare

Made a round mask of our each sleep-dazed face,
Bodiless, or else bodied by horses
That whinnied and bit and cannoned the world
        from its place.

The tall palace was so white, the moon was so round,
Everything else this plunging of horses
To the rim of our eyes that strove for the shapes
        of the sound.

We crouched at our lantern, our bodies drank the din,
And we longed for a death trampled by such horses
As every grain of the earth had hooves and mane.

We must have fallen like drunkards into a dream
Of listening, lulled by the thunder of the horses.
We awoke stiff; broad day had come.

Out through the gate the unprinted desert stretched
To stone and scorpion; our stable-horses
Lay in their straw, in a hag-sweat, listless and wretched.

Now let us, tied, be quartered by these poor horses,
If but doomsday's flames be great horses,
The forever itself a circling of the hooves of horses.

PONIES

Carved out of the darkness and far below
In the very last working, a stable
Where the pressure transforms into trees
Pit-props, rosettes into sunflowers,
Into grazing nosebags and the droppings
That smoulder among lumps of coal.

Like the fuzzy star her forelock covers,
A yarn about a townland somewhere –
Two fields and no more, in one of them
The convergence of three counties, and her
Standing up to the gaskins in foxgloves,
Agrimony, swaying meadowsweet.

MICHAEL LONGLEY   59

TWO HORSES

On a warm night in June
I went to the lake, got on all fours,
and drank like an animal. Two horses
came up beside me to drink as well.
This is amazing, I thought, but who will believe it?
The horses eyed me from time to time, snorting
and nodding. I felt the need to respond, so I snorted,
     too,
but haltingly, as though not really wanting to be heard.
The horses must have sensed that I was holding back.
They moved slightly away. Then I thought they might
     have known me
in another life – the one in which I was a poet.
They might have even read my poems, for back then,
in that shadowy time when our eagerness knew
     no bounds,
we changed styles almost as often as there were days
     in the year.

ALL SHALL BE RESTORED

The grains shall be collected
from the thousand shores
to which they found their way,
and the boulder restored,
and the boulder itself replaced
in the cliff, and likewise
the cliff shall rise
or subside until the plate of earth
is without fissure. Restoration
knows no half measure. It will
not stop when the treasured and lost
bronze horse remounts the steps.
Even this horse will founder backward
to coin, cannon, and domestic pots,
which themselves shall bubble and
drain back to green veins in stone.
And every word written shall lift off
letter by letter, the backward text
read ever briefer, ever more antic
in its effort to insist that nothing
shall be lost.

KAY RYAN   61

HORSE IN THE CAGE

Its face, as long as an arm, looks down & down.
Then the iron gate sound of the cage swings shut
above the bed, a bell as big as the room: quarter-
moon of the head, its nose, its whole lean body
pressed against its cell . . .
I watched my father hit a horse in the face once.
It had come down to feed across the fence.
My father, this stranger, wanted to ride.
Perhaps he only wanted to talk. Anyway,
he hit the ground and something broke.
As a child I never understood how an animal
could sleep standing. In my dream the horse
rocks in a cage too small, so the cage swings.
I still wake up dreaming, in front of a long face.
That day I hugged the ground hard.
Who knows if my heartbroken father was meant
to last longer than his last good drunk.
They say it's like being kicked by a horse.
You go down, your knees hug up.
You go suddenly wide awake, and the gate shuts.

HORSES

A sky. A field. A hedge flagrant with gorse.
I'm trying to remember, as best I can,
if I'm a man dreaming I'm a plowhorse
or a great plowhorse dreaming I'm a man.

Midsummer eve. St. John's wort. Spleenwort. Spurge.
I'm hard on the heels of the sage, Chuang Tzu,
when he slips into what was once a forge
through a door in the shape of a horseshoe.

RIDER

This time we are getting drunk on retsina
in somebody's Italian backyard. We are a long way
    from Georgia
and all of us are lonely. I wave my arms
and caw like Hadrian after his lover drowned himself.
My wife walks by the pond singing a hymn;
I think she is leaving me for good. I say, Imagine
my heart is huge and has
    little men
walking around inside. They don't know each other
but they're stuck there eternally
and have to get along. One of them starts shouting;
he finds a black horse and rides it around in a circle.
The others laugh at him. He leaps from the horse and
starts to choke the smallest man. Something like a hand
    starts pumping the heart
and the men nearly go crazy from the pressure.
– The first olive I picked from a tree
was so bitter I nearly threw up. My wife is strolling
around this strange landscape full of broken pediments
as if she plans to be happy from now on. I think
I have to tense it up, act like I'm in control.
I don't think I can do that. In a few hours the sun will
rise over my brother's backyard in south Georgia.
He'll come out and admire the water jewels

the night has hung in the kumquat bush. He'll hear his
        son say, 'Mama,
it's too big for me to wear,' and remember quitting the
        baseball team thirty years ago
and wish again he hadn't.
– I get up and march down to the pond. I start to speak
        to my wife
but then I feel a hand
that is about to crush my heart.

A CAT, A HORSE AND THE SUN

a cat mistrusts the sun
keeps out of its way
only where sun and shadow meet
it moves

a horse loves the sun
it basks all day
snorts
and beats its hooves

the sun likes horses
but hates cats
that is why it makes hay
and heats tin roofs

THE DEATH OF MYTH-MAKING

Two virtues ride, by stallion, by nag,
    To grind our knives and scissors:
Lantern-jawed Reason, squat Common Sense,
One courting doctors of all sorts,
    One, housewives and shopkeepers.

The trees are lopped, the poodles trim,
    The laborer's nails pared level
Since those two civil servants set
Their whetstone to the blunted edge
    And minced the muddling devil

Whose owl-eyes in the scraggly wood
    Scared mothers to miscarry,
Drove the dogs to cringe and whine,
And turned the farmboy's temper wolfish,
    The housewife's, desultory.

MEDLEY FOR MORIN KHUR

The sound box is made of a horse's head.
The resonator is horse skin.
The strings and bow are of horsehair.

The morin khur is the thoroughbred
of Mongolian violins.
Its call is the call of the stallion to the mare.

A call which may no more be gainsaid
than that of jinn to jinn
through jasmine-weighted air.

A call that may no more be gainsaid
than that of blood kin to kin
through a body-strewn central square.

A square in which they'll heap the horses' heads
by the heaps of horse skin
and the heaps of horsehair.

THE CROWDS CHEERED AS GLOOM GALLOPED AWAY

Everyone was happier. But where did the sadness go? People wanted to know. They didn't want it collecting in their elbows or knees then popping up later. The girl who thought of the ponies made a lot of money. Now a month's supply of pills came in a hard blue case with a handle. You opened it & found the usual vial plus six tiny ponies of assorted shapes & sizes, softly breathing in the Styrofoam. Often they had to be pried out & would wobble a little when first put on the ground. In the beginning the children tried to play with them, but the sharp hooves nicked their fingers & the ponies refused to jump over pencil hurdles. The children stopped feeding them sugar water & the ponies were left to break their legs on the gardens' gravel paths or drown in the gutters. On the first day of the month, rats gathered on doorsteps & spat out only the bitter manes. Many a pony's last sight was a bounding squirrel with its tail hovering over its head like a halo. Behind the movie theatre the hardier ponies gathered in packs amongst the cigarette butts, getting their hooves stuck in wads of gum. They lined the hills at funerals, huddled under folding chairs at weddings. It became a matter of pride if one of your ponies proved unusually sturdy. People would smile & say, 'This would have been an awful month for me,' pointing to the glossy palomino trotting energetically around their ankles. Eventually, the ponies were no longer needed. People had learned to imagine their sadness trotting away. & when they wanted something more tangible, they could always go to the racetrack & study the larger horses' faces. Gloom, #341, with those big black eyes, was almost sure to win.

ARS POETICA

I wander and wander.
There are paths and there are horses.
There are notebooks and notebooks full of
      handwritten words
where people have wondered their thoughts across
      lines.
Yes, I have been known to make some mistakes.
I have taken myself some places I shouldn't have,
      and I've always been glad.
I shall keep on wandering until I die
although sometimes I feel sick and have to lie down
      for a couple days.
Sometimes I dream of getting tattoos and regretting it.
Sometimes sex tricks me into love, and sometimes love
      tricks me into sex,
but I don't mind for long.
My horse looks like a few red streaks someone painted
      in the air.
I'm always surprised when she holds my weight.
Let's kiss goodbye before I climb up and ride on.
I'm grateful to have met you.

I LOVE THEM AS I'M
DEFYING THEM

I am the new colt.
I took the creamery road to the palace.
I took the chill-knob to be polished.
It was a lonely way.

My underside is beige and surprising
as the belly of a fire truck.
I took the creamery road.
I took the palace.

Tearing the grass with my black feet
I struck at the night with my firetruck neck
and found it once, the palace.

I am in it now alone.
I am precious like rosacea.
I stand for youth on my new knees
and I carried this flag the whole way.

I am several.
I am not harmless. I am small horses.

THE TRUTH

And now,
the horse is entering
the sea, and the sea
                    holds it.

Where are we?

Behind us,
the beach,
            yes, its

scrim,
        yes, of
                    grass, dune, sky – Desire

goes by, and though
it's wind of course making
the grass bend,

                    unbend, we say
it's desire again, passing
us by, souveniring us with
gospel the grass, turned
choir, leans into,

Coming –
Lord, soon.

Because
it still matters, to say something. Like:
the heart isn't

      really breakable,
not in the way you mean, any more
than a life shatters,

      – which is what
dropped shells can do, or a bond sworn to,
remember, once

      couldn't, a wooden boat between
unmanageable wave and rock or,
as hard, the shore.

The wooden boat is
not the heart,
      the wave the flesh,
          the rock the soul –

and if we thought so, we have merely been
that long
mistaken.

           Also,
about the shore: it doesn't
mean all trespass
is forgiven, if nightly
the sand is cleared of
any sign
           we were here.

It doesn't equal that whether
we were here or not
matters,
doesn't –

           Waves, because
so little of the world, even
when we say that it has
shifted, has:

same voices,
ghosts, same
hungers come,
           stop coming –
Soon –

How far the land can be found to
be, and
of a sudden,

                    sometimes. Now –
so far from rest,
should rest be needed –

Will it drown?

The horse, I mean.

And I – who do not ride, and
do not swim

And would that I had never climbed
its back

And love you too

PRAYER

As I hold my head low
I see the many flecks of black pepper
on my placemat.
They look like horses
running away from me at a great distance.

A PROGRESSION OF SCENTS

Woke up one day as a horse.
Never suspected it.
Didn't even dream that fear.

But I missmelled horsey. Hair,
hay, leather – the long strands hanging
stably on the wall –
bring me the very room, another self,
the barn a cozy bed, and every scent
in place, though no clear sight.

My hand alights a moment
on the stall door.
The other side I'm pounding
with my hoofs,
such splintering sound.

THE HORSE'S ADVENTURE

The horse discovered a gateway to another
dimension, and with nothing else to do, moseyed
into it just for grins, and man, you
don't even want to know what happened
next – it was just, like, Horse at the French
Revolution. Horse in Franco's living room.
Horse on the moon. Horse in a supporting role
in an episode of ER. Horse being shot
out of a cannon. Horse on The Price Is Right.
Horse in a Whitesnake video. Horse
at Kennedy's assassination. Horse in the Tet
Offensive. Horse at the Gap gawking at some
khaki pants. Horse in Julie Piepmeyer's
bathroom. Horse being tossed out of an airplane
with a parachute strapped to its back, plummeting
toward Nebraska. Horse on Capitol Hill
(Yes, I'd like the floor to recognize
the distinguished horse from Arizona). Horse
on the subway. Horse authorizing a peace treaty
between the U.S. and Iraq. Horse
in the Evansville State Hospital. Horse caught up
in a White Hen robbery. Horse in the Kentucky
Derby. Horse staring at the merry-go-round
at King's Island in Cincinnati, Ohio.
The list goes on and on. And so goes

the horse's adventure, where one minute
it's standing next to Pat Sajak and with a violent
flash like that of a murderous camera or the twirling
screen and music of a Batman episode
it's standing in the middle of US-23
with a screaming motorist speeding toward it.
And this horse, whirling through dimension
after dimension, spiraling carmines, suicidal
jasmines, and mathematical theorems tornadoing
past it, being placed in situation
after situation – what had it learned
when all was said and done and it was back
at Tom Wallace's farm? Nothing is better
than Rachel Wallace while they stand in the barn
in the middle of February and she draws pictures of it
to take to school tomorrow.

THE BRAMBLE

They lived in a hollow majestic
house, in one room, in the winter,
each with long black hair
and that is almost all I remember
of their appearance, walking out
into the sloping field
with the two remaining
horses, into the bramble
of red berries like sparks
on a contained fire.
Or why not a loose fire,
silently obeying
a law of stillness, on its back,
in the cold field?
'Why would we want to marry,'
they would say, 'when we've seen
our parents fall apart?'
The old house was mostly empty.
'It does wonders for the imagination,'
they said, 'to move through empty rooms.'

ERICA EHRENBERG   81

SELBSTGESPRÄCH MIT FRANZISKUS
(Internal monologue with Francis)

Look here: I know they were bored
stiff. Also, expecting food. And when I blew
into their nostrils, they didn't really think

> I always thought
> I had a wild side
> something that rolled its *rrr*'s
> and roamed ravenous searching
> for anything so ecstatic
> it would make surrender
> the only
> obvious choice
>
> but if I have an alter ego
> I am afraid it is mostly *Hausfrau*

they didn't really think
I was telling them secrets. *Liebe
geht durch den Magen.* But the tan one
(uneven cut on her forehead
frozen pale pink, which will fill
eventually with white hair) stayed
past nosing my coat,
let me rub the narrow bones

above her nostrils, scratch an itch
in the hollow

> what if I
> could hear them
> outside my window
> whimpering what if
> there were nothing
> at all I
> could do what
> if there were
> would I in
> the night even
> if it meant
> I'd be standing
> barely able beaten
> with them as
> night ends tomorrow
> our moans *Flügel*
> *der Morgenröte*

hollow of her throat, press
my fingers in small circles
down the ridge of her mane   *kraulen*

is the word I mean – and stepped
closer, eyes half closed,

> In the gospels, when a rich
> young ruler comes to Jesus, asks
> What must I do other than keep
> God's law, Jesus says Sell all you have,
> then follow me. The man in the gospel
> leaves, crestfallen. Franz, you stayed:
> of course it was mostly your father's,
> what you sold, and without asking
> which seems somewhat problematic,
> though when you relinquished
> your inheritance I think that counts.
> Bales of silk and brocade,
> the beautiful stuff they stitched
> into robes for priests

half closed, arched her neck
over the fence and moved her lips
toward my shoulder to reciprocate. I swiveled
slightly out of range – fillies will put teeth
into massage. The tall one with the profile
of a mule nosed in. In summer

(Probably it is not true about the wolf
you tamed, the one who was tearing
live people limb from limb and then
eating them and when you came
to that town they said Please do not go
you will die but you went
to the woods, spoke sense to him, said Be
at peace I will provide you with food
from now on. So the dogs
did not bark when the wolf
went door to door
eating scraps, and he died
two years later of old age)

In summer he will be coal-color, sleek. Here
in the evening light his winter hairs glow red
before they come to their black tips. Sun
pours through his ice-gray lens – such

    You went naked to the woods
    a scandal a crazy a smiling
    silent boy tending lepers, unfazed
    utterly by the taunts; Frenchie
    they'd called you before but now
    Fiancé of Poverty, and if
    we call Her holy today it is at least
    partly your fault

though you'd say you only loved
what was beautiful; but how
is it beautiful to go about in burlap
barefoot in snow rebuilding tiny churches

and how was it that your friends, fops, sons
of rich men too, began to straggle
to your homemade building site,
take off their shoes

such big eyes you have, so clear, lashes little wings
along the lid – he's headshy but keeps coming back

I cannot stop thinking about you
how cold you must be at night
how hunger has deepened
past emptiness, a trembling pledge,
weakness the weakness of love,
each wound a place to start anew

I line my windowsills
with potted plants
and if I go out
I wear well-padded
winter boots

I am embarrassed
when I think of you

back to breathe, close
and closer so long
as I keep my hands off.
Steam from our lungs
between us, sun reddening
toward earth's hungry curve

I LOST MY HORSE

I was looking for an animal, calf or lamb,
in the wire, metal and hair along the fence line.
Wire, metal and hair and there, in the gully, a man

I was pretending was dead. I pretended
to leave him where the woods met the meadow,
walking fast because I'd left my horse lashed

to a fence I lost track of two valleys
ago. Like a horse, I shied from the dead.
Here, calf. Here, lamb. I listened, wanting

(without my horse, my calf or lamb) to be
whipsmart rather than wanted. I wore orange
on antelope season's first afternoon

and waited for the click that means the safety is
off. When I spoke, my story was about picking
skulls clean. I wanted everything to be

afraid of me, the horseless girl who wanted
to kill a dead man again. The white bed
with a window behind its headboard became

ice on the meadow road and a tree to stop
a truck dead. I meant to trace my boot steps
back to the fence where things went wrong,

find my horse mouthing the bit, tied up by her
reins. I looked for the horse because she looked
safe enough to love. I looked for the calf

or lamb because there was no calf or lamb.
The man left before I could leave him, and I pretended
the world was afraid of me because I was alone.

From THE HORSE FAIR

My skirts would have been a great hindrance, making me
conspicuous and perhaps calling forth unpleasant remarks.
... Thus I was taken for a young lad, and unmolested.

ROSA BONHEUR

Found out, identified astride
the chestnut, head tilted
in the manner of the rearing

gray Percheron, you are
Rosa Bonheur disguised as one
of the handlers,

cross-dressed in a blue smock,
center of the painting.
You are performing a fantasy

of belonging
to a genre-scene that admits
none of your sex

and now the art history
that permitted you
to remain invisible

finds you androgynous
where horses bristle
at their restraining tack.

There is in every animal's eye a dim image and gleam of
humanity, a flash of strange light through which their life
looks out and up to our great mystery of command over them.
                                                    JOHN RUSKIN

She would not see them as subservient.
She painted the tarsal joint of the hind leg
for forty years, perfecting its voluted spring.
She knew the Arabian horse to be of porphyry,
        granite, and sandstone;
she knew the English stallion Hobgoblin, veined with
        seawater.
She knew anatomical science predicted movement;
thus, in trousers and boots, through the
        slaughterhouses and stockyards
and livestock markets, a small woman with cropped
        hair passed.
She knew the Belgian, her dense ossature, wattage of
        the livid eye,
oscillation of gait, the withheld stampede gathering
in the staunch shoulder for the haulage of artillery.
She would not picture subservience.

I have a veritable passion, you know, for this
        unfortunate race
and I deplore that it is disappearing before the White
usurpers.

ROSA BONHEUR

Cody sold *the unfortunate race* to England and France
as the *real* west in *actual scenes*
of slaughters in which he bragged he had taken part
we do not know – the facts
surrounding his life are uncertain

but not the promotional posters with Red Shirt
and Rosa Bonheur
given permission to draw in the thirty-acre field
where performers camped
between staged conquests Cody presented as *civilizing*

A chronicle of despair said Black Elk who joined
The Rough Riders to mend the broken
hoop of history   In the portrait Bonheur painted
Cody rides a white horse, sits tall in fringed buckskin
on playbills and postcards

They say he was not entirely pleased with the likeness
and had his head repainted

Now I am turned 73 and have only one tooth left
        wherewith
to snarl at humanity.

ROSA BONHEUR

Nine horses running in a cadenced score,
their unshod hooves thresh the wheat and the
        thresher's whip
like a high note on the unfinished canvas.

An immense dream of balance, gallop, and pivot —
without bridle or harness —
the picture hung for thirty years in the atelier.

She wanted to show the fire that blows
from the horses' nostrils, and the driven herd
        mutinous, rising
and falling along the enclosure of the thresher's will

into the foundry of weight and motion
where metal melts and pours into horse.
Dangerous as fission the arson of their turning,

tails flare behind obdurate haunches, chests brace in
    disavowal.
She painted the intelligence of dished faces resisting –
her life's project their refusal.

A LOVE SUPREME

You beautiful, broke-
back horse of my heart. Proud,
debonair, not quite there

in the head. You current
with no river in sight.
Current as confetti

after parades. You
small-town. Italian
ice shop next to brothels

beside the highway.
Sweet and sweaty. You high
as a kite coming

down. You suburban sprawled
on the bed. You dead? Not
nearly. Not yet.

RIPRAP

Lay down these words
Before your mind like rocks.
        placed solid, by hands
In choice of place, set
Before the body of the mind
        in space and time:
Solidity of bark, leaf, or wall
        riprap of things:
Cobble of milky way,
        straying planets,
These poems, people,
        lost ponies with
Dragging saddles –
        and rocky sure-foot trails.
The worlds like an endless
        four-dimensional
Game of *Go*.
        ants and pebbles
In the thin loam, each rock a word
        a creek-washed stone
Granite: ingrained
        with torment of fire and weight
Crystal and sediment linked hot
        all change, in thoughts,
As well as things.

'DON'T LET THAT HORSE'

Don't let that horse
                    eat that violin

    cried Chagall's mother

                        But he
            kept right on
                        painting

And became famous

And kept on painting
                    The Horse With Violin In Mouth
And when he finally finished it
he jumped up upon the horse
                        and rode away
            waving the violin

And then with a low bow gave it
to the first naked nude he ran across

And there were no strings
                        attached

LAWRENCE FERLINGHETTI   97

ON THE FARM,
OFF TO THE HUNT

THE DUSK OF HORSES

Right under their noses, the green
Of the field is paling away
Because of something fallen from the sky.

They see this, and put down
Their long heads deeper in grass
That only just escapes reflecting them

As the dream of a millpond would.
The color green flees over the grass
Like an insect, following the red sun over

The next hill. The grass is white.
There is no cloud so dark and white at once;
There is no pool at dawn that deepens

Their faces and thirsts as this does.
Now they are feeding on solid
Cloud, and, one by one,

With nails as silent as stars among the wood
Hewed down years ago and now rotten,
The stalls are put up around them.

JAMES DICKEY   101

HAY FOR THE HORSES

He had driven half the night
From far down San Joaquin
Through Mariposa, up the
Dangerous Mountain roads,
And pulled in at eight a.m.
With his big truckload of hay
    behind the barn.
With winch and ropes and hooks
We stacked the bales up clean
To splintery redwood rafters
High in the dark, flecks of alfalfa
Whirling through shingle-cracks of light,
Itch of haydust in the
    sweaty shirt and shoes.
At lunchtime under Black oak
Out in the hot corral,
– The old mare nosing lunchpails,
Grasshoppers crackling in the weeds –
'I'm sixty-eight' he said,
'I first bucked hay when I was seventeen.
I thought, that day I started,
I sure would hate to do this all my life.
And dammit, that's just what
I've gone and done.'

FOR THE NIGHT

The mare kicks
in her darkening stall, knocks
over a bucket.

The goose ...

The cow keeps a peaceful brain
behind her broad face.

Last light moves
through cracks in the wall,
over bales of hay.

And the bat lets
go of the rafter, falls
into black air.

IN THE UPPER PASTURE

In the evergreen grove that abuts the pasture we are
limbing low branches, carting away deadwood,
cutting close to the trunk so the sap does not bleed,
to make a shelter, a run-in for foals and their mares.
We will not shorten the lives of these hemlocks
    and pines
in the afternoon of our own lives, yet I am sad
to think that the dell will outlast us and our bloodlines.

Is this a pastoral? Be not deceived
by the bellows of leathery teats giving suck,
by the fringe of delicate beard that pricks
its braille notes on the muzzle of the newborn.
When instinct whinnies between dam and foal
at night in the rain, do not be lulled.
Each of us whimpers his way through the forest alone.

With scrap lumber we patiently fence off
a triad of trees that have grown so close to each other
a young horse darting through might be taken prisoner.
Let the babies be safe here, let them lie down on
    pine duff
away from the merciless blackflies, out of the weather.
Under the latticework of old trees let me stand
pitch-streaked and pleasured by this small thing we
    have done.

FOLLOWER

My father worked with a horse-plough,
His shoulders globed like a full sail strung
Between the shafts and the furrow.
The horses strained at his clicking tongue.

An expert. He would set the wing
And fit the bright steel-pointed sock.
The sod rolled over without breaking.
At the headrig, with a single pluck

Of reins, the sweating team turned round
And back into the land. His eye
Narrowed and angled at the ground,
Mapping the furrow exactly.

I stumbled in his hobnailed wake,
Fell sometimes on the polished sod;
Sometimes he rode me on his back
Dipping and rising to his plod.

I wanted to grow up and plough,
To close one eye, stiffen my arm.
All I ever did was follow
In his broad shadow round the farm.

I was a nuisance, tripping, falling,
Yapping always. But today
It is my father who keeps stumbling
Behind me, and will not go away.

SEAMUS HEANEY   105

NIGHT-PIECE

Must you know it again?
Dull pounding through hay,
The uneasy whinny.

A sponge lip drawn off each separate tooth.
Opalescent haunch,
Muscle and hoof

Bundled under the roof.

THE SOLITARY HUNTSMAN

The solitary huntsman
No coat of pink doth wear,
But midnight black from cap to spur
Upon his midnight mare.
He drones a tuneless jingle
In lieu of tally-ho:
'I'll catch a fox
And put him in a box
And never let him go.'
The solitary huntsman,
He follows silent hounds.
No horn proclaims his joyless sport,
And never a hoofbeat sounds.
His hundred hounds, his thousands,
Their master's will they know:
To catch a fox
And put him in a box
And never let him go.
For all the fox's doubling
They track him to his den.
The chase may fill a morning,
Or threescore years and ten.
The huntsman never sated
Screaks to his saddlebow,
'I'll catch another fox
And put him in a box
And never let him go.'

'THE HUNTSMEN, ON TOP OF THEIR SWAYING HORSE-TOWERS'

The huntsmen, on top of their swaying horse-towers,
Faces raw as butcher's blocks, are angry.
They have lost their fox.

They have lost most of their hounds.
I can't help.

The one I hunt
The one
I shall rend to pieces
Whose blood I shall dab on your cheek

Is under my coat.

PAWNEE DUST

Goodbye, I see the horsemen mounting,
the lean dogs yapping in the dust.
Cottonwood pole and buffalo hide
are rolled and lashed, Gray Eagle's
woman carries the smoldering fire.

The young are laughing, they have no
burden yet, the broken camp is play.

Goodbye, the sun already rises,
bones of the last hunt whiten
in its rays. The plains are there
before you, beyond are grass
and water, vast untroubled herds.

Great Tirawa watches you, there's
nothing more to say. Good hunting west.

WAR HORSES

ÆNEAS TELLS OF THE TROJAN HORSE
From the Æneid

By destiny compell'd, and in despair,
The Greeks grew weary of the tedious war,
And by Minerva's aid a fabric rear'd,
Which like a steed of monstrous height appear'd:
The sides were plank'd with pine; they feign'd it made
For their return, and this the vow they paid
Thus they pretend, but in the hollow side
Selected numbers of their soldiers hide:
With inward arms the dire machine they load,
And iron bowels stuff the dark abode.
In sight of Troy lies Tenedos, an isle
(While Fortune did on Priam's empire smile)
Renown'd for wealth; but, since, a faithless bay,
Where ships expos'd to wind and weather lay.
There was their fleet conceal'd. We thought,
        for Greece
Their sails were hoisted, and our fears release.
The Trojans, coop'd within their walls so long,
Unbar their gates, and issue in a throng,
Like swarming bees, and with delight survey
The camp deserted, where the Grecians lay:
The quarters of the sev'ral chiefs they show'd;
Here Phœnix, here Achilles, made abode;
Here join'd the battles; there the navy rode.

Part on the pile their wond'ring eyes employ:
The pile by Pallas rais'd to ruin Troy.
Thymœtes first ('tis doubtful whether hir'd,
Or so the Trojan destiny requir'd)
Mov'd that the ramparts might be broken down,
To lodge the monster fabric in the town.
But Capys, and the rest of sounder mind,
The fatal present to the flames design'd,
Or to the wat'ry deep; at least to bore
The hollow sides, and hidden frauds explore.
The giddy vulgar, as their fancies guide,
With noise say nothing, and in parts divide.
Laocoon, follow'd by a num'rous crowd,
Ran from the fort, and cried, from far, aloud:
'O wretched countrymen! what fury reigns?
What more than madness has possess'd your brains?
Think you the Grecians from your coasts are gone?
And are Ulysses' arts no better known?
This hollow fabric either must inclose,
Within its blind recess, our secret foes;
Or 'tis an engine rais'd above the town,
T' o'erlook the walls, and then to batter down.
Somewhat is sure design'd, by fraud or force:
Trust not their presents, nor admit the horse.'
Thus having said, against the steed he threw
His forceful spear, which, hissing as it flew,
Pierc'd thro' the yielding planks of jointed wood,

And trembling in the hollow belly stood.
The sides, transpierc'd, return a rattling sound,
And groans of Greeks inclos'd come issuing thro'
    the wound.
And, had not Heav'n the fall of Troy design'd,
Or had not men been fated to be blind,
Enough was said and done t' inspire a better mind.
Then had our lances pierc'd the treach'rous wood,
And Ilian tow'rs and Priam's empire stood.

INSIDE THE GOOD IDEA

From the outside it is singular. One wooden horse. Inside ten men sit cross-legged, knees touching. No noun has been invented yet to describe this. They whisper that it would be like sitting in a wine barrel if the curved walls were painted red. The contents are not content. They would like some wine. They quarrel about who gets to sit in the head until finally the smallest man clambers in, promising to send messages back to the belly. He can only look out of one eye at a time. At first there is nothing to report. Black, Dark, The Occasional Star. Then Quiet Footsteps mixed with Questions. The children are clamoring for it to be brought inside the walls. The head sends back another message which gets caught in the throat: *They are bringing their toy horses to pay their respects to us, brushing their tiny manes, oiling the little wheels. It must be a welcome change from playing war.*

ACHILLES OVER THE TRENCH
From the Iliad

Then rose Achilles dear to Zeus; and round
The warrior's puissant shoulders Pallas flung
Her fringèd ægis, and around his head
The glorious goddess wreathed a golden cloud,
And from it lighted an all-shining flame.
As when a smoke from a city goes to heaven
Far off from out an island girt by foes,
All day the men contend in grievous war
From their own city, but with set of sun
Their fires flame thickly, and aloft the glare
Flies streaming, if perchance the neighbours round
May see, and sail to help them in the war;
So from his head the splendour went to heaven.
From wall to dyke he stept, he stood, nor joined
The Achæans – honouring his wise mother's word –
There standing, shouted, and Pallas far away
Called; and a boundless panic shook the foe.
For like the clear voice when a trumpet shrills,
Blown by the fierce beleaguerers of a town,
So rang the clear voice of Æakidês;
And when the brazen cry of Æakidês
Was heard among the Trojans, all their hearts
Were troubled, and the full-maned horses whirled
The chariots backward, knowing griefs at hand;

And sheer-astounded were the charioteers
To see the dread, unweariable fire
That always o'er the great Peleion's head
Burned, for the bright-eyed goddess made it burn.
Thrice from the dyke he sent his mighty shout,
Thrice backward reeled the Trojans and allies;
And there and then twelve of their noblest died
Among their spears and chariots.

TRANS. ALFRED, LORD TENNYSON

KNOWING ABOUT HORSES
From Georgics, Book III

Like diligence requires the courser's race,
In early choice, and for a longer space.
The colt that for a stallion is design'd
By sure presages shows his generous kind;
Of able body, sound of limb and wind.
Upright he walks, on pasterns firm and straight;
His motions easy; prancing in his gait;
The first to lead the way, to tempt the flood,
To pass the bridge unknown, nor fear the
    trembling wood;
Dauntless at empty noises; lofty neck'd,
Sharp-headed, barrel-bellied, broadly back'd;
Brawny his chest, and deep; his colour grey;
For beauty, dappled, or the brightest bay:
Faint white and dun will scarce the rearing pay.
   The fiery courser, when he hears from far
The sprightly trumpets and the shouts of war,
Pricks up his ears; and, trembling with delight,
Shifts place, and paws, and hopes the promis'd fight.
On his right shoulder his thick mane, reclin'd,
Ruffles at speed, and dances in the wind.
His horny hoofs are jetty black and round;
His chine is double; starting, with a bound
He turns the turf, and shakes the solid ground.
Fire from his eyes, clouds from his nostrils flow:
He bears his rider headlong on the foe.

VIRGIL   119
TRANS. JOHN DRYDEN

From HENRY V

CONSTABLE Tut! I have the best armour of the world. Would it were day!

ORLEANS You have an excellent armour; but let my horse have his due.

CONSTABLE It is the best horse of Europe.

ORLEANS Will it never be morning?

DAUPHIN My Lord of Orleans, and my Lord High Constable, you talk of horse and armour?

ORLEANS You are as well provided of both as any prince in the world.

DAUPHIN What a long night is this! I will not change my horse with any that treads but on four pasterns. Ça, ha! he bounds from the earth, as if his entrails were hairs; le cheval volant, the Pegasus, chez les narines de feu! When I bestride him, I soar, I am a hawk. He trots the air. The earth sings when he touches it. The basest horn of his hoof is more musical than the pipe of Hermes.

ORLEANS He's of the colour of the nutmeg.

DAUPHIN And of the heat of the ginger. It is a beast for Perseus: he is pure air and fire; and the dull elements of earth and water never appear in him, but only in patient stillness while his rider mounts him. He is indeed a horse, and all other jades you may call beasts.

CONSTABLE Indeed, my lord, it is a most absolute and excellent horse.

DAUPHIN It is the prince of palfreys. His neigh is like the bidding of a monarch, and his countenance enforces homage.

ORLEANS No more, cousin.

DAUPHIN Nay, the man hath no wit that cannot, from the rising of the lark to the lodging of the lamb, vary deserved praise on my palfrey. It is a theme as fluent as the sea. Turn the sands into eloquent tongues, and my horse is argument for them all. 'Tis a subject for a sovereign to reason on, and for a sovereign's sovereign to ride on; and for the world, familiar to us and unknown, to lay apart their particular functions and wonder at him. I once writ a sonnet in his praise and began thus, 'Wonder of nature!'

ORLEANS I have heard a sonnet begin so to one's mistress.

DAUPHIN Then did they imitate that which I composed to my courser, for my horse is my mistress.

ORLEANS Your mistress bears well.

DAUPHIN Me well, which is the prescript praise and perfection of a good and particular mistress.

CONSTABLE Nay, for methought yesterday your mistress shrewdly shook your back.

DAUPHIN So perhaps did yours.

CONSTABLE Mine was not bridled.

DAUPHIN O, then belike she was old and gentle, and you rode like a kern of Ireland, your French hose off, and in your strait strossers.

CONSTABLE You have good judgement in horsemanship.

DAUPHIN Be warned by me then. They that ride so, and ride not warily, fall into foul bogs. I had rather have my horse to my mistress.

GLAUCUS

It went without saying that a king of Corinth
should keep his prize fillies out of the fray
and, rather than have them enmesh
themselves in horse toils, horse tattle,

set them up, each on a plinth,
and fillet their manes with knots and nosegays
and feed them the choicest human flesh
to give them a taste for battle.

It went without saying that after he lost control
of his chariot team at Pelias, and made a hames
of setting them all square,

Glaucus was still on such a roll
it was lost on him that the high point of the games
was his being eaten now by his own mares.

WAR GOD'S HORSE SONG

I am the Turquoise Woman's son.
On top of Belted Mountain
beautiful horses – slim like a weasel!
My horse with a hoof like a striped agate,
with his fetlock like a fine eagle plume:
my horse whose legs are like quick lightning
whose body is an eagle-plumed arrow:
my horse whose tail is like a trailing black cloud.
The Little Holy Wind blows thru his hair.
My horse with a mane made of short rainbows.
My horse with ears made of round corn.
My horse with eyes made of big stars.
My horse with a head made of mixed waters.
My horse with teeth made of white shell.
The long rainbow is in his mouth for a bridle
                and with it I guide him.
When my horse neighs, different-colored horses follow.
When my horse neighs, different-colored sheep follow.
                I am wealthy because of him.

                Before me peaceful
                Behind me peaceful
                Under me peaceful
                Over me peaceful –
                Peaceful voice when he neighs.
I am everlasting and peaceful.
I stand for my horse.

124   ANON.
      TRANS. LOUIS WATCHMAN

THE CHARGE OF THE LIGHT BRIGADE

Half a league, half a league,
Half a league onward,
All in the valley of Death
   Rode the six hundred.
'Forward, the Light Brigade!
Charge for the guns!' he said.
Into the valley of Death
   Rode the six hundred.

'Forward, the Light Brigade!'
Was there a man dismayed?
Not though the soldier knew
   Someone had blundered.
Theirs not to make reply,
Theirs not to reason why,
Theirs but to do and die.
Into the valley of Death
   Rode the six hundred.

Cannon to right of them,
Cannon to left of them,
Cannon in front of them
   Volleyed and thundered;
Stormed at with shot and shell,

Boldly they rode and well,
Into the jaws of Death,
Into the mouth of hell
    Rode the six hundred.

Flashed all their sabres bare,
Flashed as they turned in air
Sab'ring the gunners there,
Charging an army, while
All the world wondered:
Plunged in the battery smoke
Right thro' the line they broke;
Cossack and Russian
Reeled from the sabre stroke
    Shattered and sundered.
Then they rode back, but not
    Not the six hundred.

Cannon to right of them,
Cannon to left of them,
Cannon behind them
    Volleyed and thundered;
Stormed at with shot and shell,
While horse and hero fell.
They that had fought so well
Came through the jaws of Death,
Back from the mouth of hell,

All that was left of them,
  Left of six hundred.

When can their glory fade?
O the wild charge they made!
  All the world wondered.
Honour the charge they made!
Honour the Light Brigade,
  Noble six hundred!

PAUL REVERE'S RIDE

Listen, my children, and you shall hear
Of the midnight ride of Paul Revere,
On the eighteenth of April, in Seventy-five;
Hardly a man is now alive
Who remembers that famous day and year.

He said to his friend, 'If the British march
By land or sea from the town to-night,
Hang a lantern aloft in the belfry arch
Of the North Church tower as a signal light, –
One, if by land, and two, if by sea;
And I on the opposite shore will be,
Ready to ride and spread the alarm
Through every Middlesex village and farm,
For the country-folk to be up and to arm.'

Then he said 'Good night!' and with muffled oar
Silently rowed to the Charlestown shore,
Just as the moon rose over the bay,
Where swinging wide at her moorings lay
The Somerset, British man-of-war;
A phantom ship, with each mast and spar
Across the moon like a prison bar,
And a huge black hulk, that was magnified
By its own reflection in the tide.

Meanwhile, his friend, through alley and street,
Wanders and watches with eager ears,
Till in the silence around him he hears
The muster of men at the barrack door,
The sound of arms, and the tramp of feet,
And the measured tread of the grenadiers,
Marching down to their boats on the shore.

Then he climbed the tower of the Old North Church,
By the wooden stairs, with stealthy tread,
To the belfry-chamber overhead,
And startled the pigeons from their perch
On the sombre rafters, that round him made
Masses and moving shapes of shade, –
By the trembling ladder, steep and tall,
To the highest window in the wall,
Where he paused to listen and look down
A moment on the roofs of the town,
And the moonlight flowing over all.

Beneath, in the churchyard, lay the dead,
In their night-encampment on the hill,
Wrapped in silence so deep and still
That he could hear, like a sentinel's tread,
The watchful night-wind, as it went

Creeping along from tent to tent,
And seeming to whisper, 'All is well!'
A moment only he feels the spell
Of the place and the hour, and the secret dread
Of the lonely belfry and the dead;
For suddenly all his thoughts are bent
On a shadowy something far away,
Where the river widens to meet the bay, –
A line of black that bends and floats
On the rising tide, like a bridge of boats.

Meanwhile, impatient to mount and ride,
Booted and spurred, with a heavy stride
On the opposite shore walked Paul Revere.
Now he patted his horse's side,
Now gazed at the landscape far and near,
Then, impetuous, stamped the earth,
And turned and tightened his saddle-girth;
But mostly he watched with eager search
The belfry-tower of the Old North Church,
As it rose above the graves on the hill,
Lonely and spectral and sombre and still.
And lo! as he looks, on the belfry's height
A glimmer, and then a gleam of light!
He springs to the saddle, the bridle he turns,
But lingers and gazes, till full on his sight
A second lamp in the belfry burns!

A hurry of hoofs in a village street,
A shape in the moonlight, a bulk in the dark,
And beneath, from the pebbles, in passing, a spark
Struck out by a steed flying fearless and fleet:
That was all! And yet, through the gloom and
    the light,
The fate of a nation was riding that night;
And the spark struck out by that steed, in his flight,
Kindled the land into flame with its heat.

He has left the village and mounted the steep,
And beneath him, tranquil and broad and deep,
Is the Mystic, meeting the ocean tides;
And under the alders, that skirt its edge,
Now soft on the sand, now loud on the ledge,
Is heard the tramp of his steed as he rides.

It was twelve by the village clock
When he crossed the bridge into Medford town.
He heard the crowing of the cock,
And the barking of the farmer's dog,
And felt the damp of the river fog,
That rises after the sun goes down.

It was one by the village clock,
When he galloped into Lexington.
He saw the gilded weathercock

Swim in the moonlight as he passed,
And the meeting-house windows, black and bare,
Gaze at him with a spectral glare,
As if they already stood aghast
At the bloody work they would look upon.

It was two by the village clock,
When he came to the bridge in Concord town.
He heard the bleating of the flock,
And the twitter of birds among the trees,
And felt the breath of the morning breeze
Blowing over the meadow, brown.
And one was safe and asleep in his bed
Who at the bridge would be first to fall,
Who that day would be lying dead,
Pierced by a British musket-ball.

You know the rest. In the books you have read,
How the British Regulars fired and fled, –
How the farmers gave them ball for ball,
From behind each fence and farm-yard wall,
Chasing the red-coats down the lane,
Then crossing the fields to emerge again
Under the trees at the turn of the road,
And only pausing to fire and load.

So through the night rode Paul Revere;
And so through the night went his cry of alarm
To every Middlesex village and farm, –
A cry of defiance and not of fear,
A voice in the darkness, a knock at the door,
And a word that shall echo forevermore!
For, borne on the night-wind of the Past,
Through all our history, to the last,
In the hour of darkness and peril and need,
The people will waken and listen to hear
The hurrying hoof-beats of that steed,
And the midnight message of Paul Revere.

A FACE-OFF IN THE CRUSADES
From Jerusalem Delivered

It was a great, a strange, and wond'rous sight,
    When front to front those noble armies met,
How every troop, how in each troop each knight
    Stood prest to move, to fight, and praise to get.
Loose in the wind waved their ensigns light,
    Trembled the plumes that on their crests were set;
Their arms, impresses, colours, gold, and stone,
'Gainst the sun-beams smil'd, flamed, sparkled, shone:

Of dry-top'd oaks they seem'd two forests thick,
    So did each host with spears and pikes abound:
Bent were their bows, in rest their lances stick,
    Their hands shook swords, their slings held
        cobles round.
Each steed to run was ready, prest, and quick
    At his commander's spur, his hand, his sound;
He chafes, he stamps, careers, and turns about;
He foams, snorts, neighs, and fire and smoke
        breathes out.

Horror itself in that fair sight seem'd fair,
    And pleasure flew amid sad dread and fear;
The trumpets shrill that thunder'd in the air
    Were music mild and sweet to every ear;

The faithful camp, though less, yet seem'd more rare
  In that strange noise, more warlike, shrill, and clear,
In notes more sweet; the pagan trumpets jar:
These sung, their armours shin'd; those glister'd far.

HOHENLINDEN

On Linden, when the sun was low,
All bloodless lay the untrodden snow,
And dark as winter was the flow
    Of Iser, rolling rapidly.

But Linden saw another sight,
When the drum beat, at dead of night,
Commanding fires of death to light
    The darkness of her scenery.

By torch and trumpet fast arrayed,
Each horseman drew his battle blade,
And furious every charger neighed
    To join the dreadful revelry.

Then shook the hills, with thunder riven;
Then rushed the steed, to battle driven;
And, louder than the bolts of heaven,
    Far flashed the red artillery.

But redder yet that light shall glow,
On Linden's hills of stainèd snow;
And bloodier yet, the torrent flow
    Of Iser, rolling rapidly.

'Tis morn; but scarce yon level sun
Can pierce the war-clouds, rolling dun,
Where furious Frank, and fiery Hun,
   Shout in their sulphurous canopy.

The combat deepens. On, ye brave,
Who rush to glory, or the grave!
Wave, Munich, all thy banners wave,
   And charge with all thy chivalry!

Few, few shall part, where many meet!
The snow shall be their winding sheet,
And every turf, beneath their feet,
   Shall be a soldier's sepulchre.

THOMAS CAMPBELL

O FLODDEN FIELD

The learned King fought
like a fool, flanked
and outtricked, who hacked
in a corner of cousins
until the ten thousand
swords lay broken,
and the women walked
in their houses alone.

On a journey among horses,
the spirit of a man who died
only a week ago
is walking through heather
and forgets that its body
had seventy years.
Wild horses are singing,
and voices of the rocks.

The spirit from the boneyard
finds a new life, in the field
where the King's wound
built the blackness of Glasgow
and the smoke of the air.
The spirit, like a boy,
picks up from the heather
a whole sword.

From RICHARD III

CATESBY *[Calling]*
 Rescue, my Lord of Norfolk, rescue, rescue!
 The king enacts more wonders than a man,
 Daring an opposite to every danger.
 His horse is slain, and all on foot he fights,
 Seeking for Richmond in the throat of death.
 Rescue, fair lord, or else the day is lost!
  Alarums. Enter [King] Richard.
KING RICHARD
 A horse, a horse! My kingdom for a horse!
CATESBY
 Withdraw, my lord. I'll help you to a horse.
KING RICHARD
 Slave, I have set my life upon a cast,
 And I will stand the hazard of the die.
 I think there be six Richmonds in the field,
 Five have I slain today instead of him.
 A horse, a horse! My kingdom for a horse!
  [Exeunt.]

WILLIAM SHAKESPEARE   139

THE WAR HORSE

This dry night, nothing unusual
About the clip, clop, casual

Iron of his shoes as he stamps death
Like a mint on the innocent coinage of earth.

I lift the window, watch the ambling feather
Of hock and fetlock, loosed from its daily tether

In the tinker camp on the Enniskerry Road,
Pass, his breath hissing, his snuffling head

Down. He is gone. No great harm is done.
Only a leaf of our laurel hedge is torn –

Of distant interest like a maimed limb,
Only a rose which now will never climb

The stone of our house, expendable, a mere
Line of defence against him, a volunteer

You might say, only a crocus, its bulbous head
Blown from growth, one of the screamless dead.

But we, we are safe, our unformed fear
Of fierce commitment gone; why should we care

If a rose, a hedge, a crocus are uprooted
Like corpses, remote, crushed, mutilated?

He stumbles on like a rumour of war, huge
Threatening. Neighbours use the subterfuge

Of curtains. He stumbles down our short street
Thankfully passing us. I pause, wait,

Then to breathe relief lean on the sill
And for a second only my blood is still

With atavism. That rose he smashed frays
Ribboned across our hedge, recalling days

Of burned countryside, illicit braid:
A cause ruined before, a world betrayed.

COWBOYS AND HORSES

GHOST TOWN

Sun gone from the evening sky,
shadows reach on the plain,
the low hills turn from brown
to purple and slowly fade;
call of sleepy quail from the sage,
the road winds west,
a man rides into the dusk.

The streets of an empty town —
they lie in a dust that only
the wind disturbs. The sun
has hammered there and the rain
driven in. Buildings lean
together, gray, loose-boarded,
creaking when the wind blows.

Turn back to see it as it was.
Horses line the street, nosing
the rails. Wagons clatter by.
Dark men in dusty clothing,
pale men dressed for business,
outnumbered women. Shouts,
coarse laughter, music from a bar.

Behind those doors men sought
their pleasure, lay with it,
gambled for it, drank it down like
water, wept and cursed when
it was gone. Murder and justice
stained the floors and soaked
into the streets; the cries of

dead men lingered at high noon.
The streets led out to hill
and plain, men came and went and
did not leave their names.
Smell of dust and sweat and dung.
The sound of booted feet on the
boards, shod hoofs and wheels.

The road winds west, the rider
fades into the dusk. Moonrise
in the east, yelp of coyote from
the sage. Darkness on the plain,
shadows and silence in the town.
The wind rises from another
morning, where the rider goes.

From THE JOLLY COWBOY

My lover, he is a cowboy, he's brave and kind and true,
He rides a Spanish pony, he throws a lasso, too;
And when he comes to see me our vows we do redeem,
He throws his arms around me and thus begins to sing:

'Ho, I'm a jolly cowboy, from Texas now I hail,
Give me my quirt and pony, I'm ready for the trail;
I love the rolling prairies, they're free from care
          and strife,
Behind a herd of longhorns I'll journey all my life.

When early dawn is breaking and we are far away,
We fall into our saddles, we round up all the day;
We rope, we brand, we ear-mark, I tell you we are smart,
And when the herd is ready, for Kansas then we start.

Oh, I am a Texas cowboy, lighthearted, brave, and free,
To roam the wide, wide prairie, 'tis always joy to me.
My trusty little pony is my companion true,
O'er creeks and hills and rivers he's sure to pull me
          through.'

ANON.   147

From LASCA

I want free life, and I want fresh air;
And I sigh for the canter after the cattle,
The crack of the whips like shots in battle,
The medley of hoofs and horns and heads
That wars and wrangles and scatters and spreads;
The green beneath and the blue above,
And dash and danger, and life and love –
And Lasca!

Lasca used to ride
On a mouse-grey mustang close to my side,
With blue serape and bright-belled spur;
I laughed with joy as I looked at her!
Little knew she of books or creeds;
An Ave Maria sufficed her needs;
Little she cared save to be at my side,
To ride with me, and ever to ride,
From San Saba's shore to Lavaca's tide.
She was as bold as the billows that beat,
She was as wild as the breezes that blow:
From her little head to her little feet,
She was swayed in her suppleness to and fro
By each gust of passion; a sapling pine
That grows on the edge of a Kansas bluff
And wars with the wind when the weather is rough,
Is like this Lasca, this love of mine.

*   *   *

Was that thunder? I grasped the cord
Of my swift mustang without a word.
I sprang to the saddle, and she clung behind.
Away! on a hot chase down the wind!
But never was foxhunt half so hard,
And never was steed so little spared.
For we rode for our lives. You shall hear how we fared
In Texas, down by the Rio Grande.

The mustang flew, and we urged him on;
There was one chance left, and you have but one –
Halt, jump to the ground, and shoot your horse;
Crouch under his carcass, and take your chance;
And if the steers in their frantic course
Don't batter you both to pieces at once,
You may thank your star; if not, goodbye
To the quickening kiss and the long-drawn sigh,
And the open air and the open sky,
In Texas, down by the Rio Grande.

FRANK DESPREZ   149

FASTER HORSES

He was an old-time cowboy, don't you understand,
His eyes were sharp as razor blades, his face was
    leather-tanned,
His toes were pointed inward from a-hangin' on a horse –
He was an old philosopher, of course.
He was so thin, I swear you could have used him for
    a whip,
He had to drink a beer to keep his britches on his hips.
I knew I had to ask him about the mysteries of life;
He spit between his boots and he replied,
'It's faster horses, younger women, older whiskey,
    more money.'

He smiled and all his teeth were covered with tobacco
    stains.
He said, 'It don't do men no good to pray for peace
    and rain.
Peace and rain is just a way to say prosperity,
And buffalo chips is all it means to me.'
I told him I was a poet, I was lookin' for the truth,
I do not care for horses, whiskey, women, or the loot.
I said I was a writer, my soul was all on fire;
He looked at me and he said, 'You are a liar.
    Son –
It's faster horses, younger women, older whiskey,
    more money.'

Well, I was disillusioned, if I say the least.
I grabbed him by the collar and I jerked him to his feet –
There was somethin' cold and shiny layin' by my head,
So I started to believe the things he said.
Well, my poet days are over and I'm back to bein' me,
As I enjoy the peace and comfort of reality.
If my son ever asks me what it is that I have learned,
I think that I will readily affirm,

    'Son –

It's faster horses, younger women, older whiskey,
    more money,
Faster horses, younger women, older whiskey,
    more money,
Faster horses, younger women, older whiskey, more money...

TOM T. HALL

THE OLD CHISHOLM TRAIL

Come along boys and listen to my tale,
I'll tell you of my troubles on the old Chisholm trail.

Come a ti yi yippee, come a ti yi yea,
Come a ti yi yippee, come a ti yi yea.

Oh, a ten-dollar hoss and a forty-dollar saddle,
And I'm goin' to punchin' Texas cattle.

I wake in the mornin' afore daylight,
And afore I sleep the moon shines bright.

It's cloudy in the west, a-lookin' like rain,
And my durned old slicker's in the wagon again.

No chaps, no slicker, and it's pourin' down rain,
And I swear, by gosh, I'll never night-herd again.

Feet in the stirrups and seat in the saddle,
I hung and rattled with them long-horn cattle.

The wind commenced to blow, and the rain began to fall,
Hit looked, by grab, like we was goin' to lose 'em all.

I don't give a darn if they never do stop;
I'll ride as long as an eight-day clock.

We rounded 'em up and put 'em on the cars,
And that was the last of the old Two Bars.

Oh, it's bacon and beans most every day,
I'd as soon be a-eatin' prairie hay.

I went to the boss to draw my roll,
He had it figgered out I was nine dollars in the hole.

Goin' back to town to draw my money,
Goin' back home to see my honey.

With my knees in the saddle and my seat in the sky,
I'll quit punchin' cows in the sweet by and by.

Come a ti yi yippee, come a ti yi yea,
Come a ti yi yippee, come a ti yi yea.

RIDIN'

There is some that like the city –
  Grass that's curried smooth and green,
Theaytres and stranglin' collars,
  Wagons run by gasoline –
But for me it's hawse and saddle
  Every day without a change,
And a desert sun a-blazin'
  On a hundred miles of range.

  Just a-ridin', a-ridin' –
    Desert ripplin' in the sun,
  Mountains blue along the skyline –
    I don't envy anyone
      When I'm ridin'.

When my feet is in the stirrups
  And my hawse is on the bust,
With his hoofs a-flashin' lightnin'
  From a cloud of golden dust,
And the bawlin' of the cattle
  Is a-comin' down the wind
Then a finer life than ridin'
  Would be mighty hard to find.

154

Just a-ridin', a-ridin' —
    Splittin' long cracks through the air,
Stirrin' up a baby cyclone,
    Rippin' up the prickly pear
        As I'm ridin'.

I don't need no art exhibits
    When the sunset does her best,
Paintin' everlastin' glory
    On the mountains to the west
And your opery looks foolish
    When the night-bird starts his tune
And the desert's silver mounted
    By the touches of the moon.

    Just a-ridin', a-ridin' —
        Who kin envy kings and czars
    When the coyotes down the valley
        Are a singin' to the stars,
            If he's ridin'?

When my earthly trail is ended
    And my final bacon curled
And the last great roundup's finished
    At the Home Ranch of the world

I don't want no harps nor haloes
    Robes nor other dressed up things –
Let me ride the starry ranges
    On a pinto hawse with wings!

    Just a-ridin', a-ridin' –
        Nothin' I'd like half so well
As a-roundin' up the sinners
        That have wandered out of Hell,
            And a-ridin'.

SCIENCE CAME WEST

They weren't all fighting men, some traded knives,
Tobacco, scarlet cloth, vermillion dye,
And rum and cakes of salt . . . and some their lives
For aster pollen and a butterfly,
Or for a star against a mountain sky
That fixed the longitude and latitude
Into a crumpled note-book carried by
A thirsty mule that crumpling would be food;
They weren't all fighting men, some gave their blood
To christen wormwood after Artemis,
To pole a perogue through a stinking flood,
To watch a warbler in the clematis . . .
Now cutting blossoms, now dead manes and tails
For girths to bind fresh horses to the trails.

THOMAS HORNSBY FERRIL   157

GIT ALONG LITTLE DOGIES

As I went a-walkin' one mornin' for pleasure,
I spied a cowpuncher come ridin' along;
His hat was throwed back and his spurs was a-jinglin'
And as he approached he was singin' this song.

Whoopee ti yi yo, git along, little dogies,
It's your misfortune and none of my own;
Whoopee ti yi yo, git along, little dogies,
You know that Wyoming will be your new home.

It's early in spring that we round up the dogies,
And mark 'em and brand 'em and bob off their tails;
We round up our horses and load the chuckwagon,
And then throw them dogies out onto the trail.

Its whoopin' and yellin' and a-drivin' them dogies,
Oh, lord, how I wish that you would go on;
It's a-whoopin' and punchin' and go on-a, little dogies,
'Cause you know that Wyoming is to be your new home.

Some cowboys go up the trail just for the pleasure,
But that's where they always go gettin' it wrong,
For nobody knows just what trouble they give us,
As we go a-drivin' them dogies along.

Whoopee ti yi yo, git along, little dogies,
It's your misfortune and none of my own;
Whoopee ti yi yo, git along, little dogies,
You know that Wyoming will be your new home.

TRADITIONAL   159

EQUINE
ENCOUNTERS

THE WHITE HORSE

The youth walks up to the white horse, to put its
    halter on
and the horse looks at him in silence.
They are so silent, they are in another world.

D. H. LAWRENCE

THE HORSES

I climbed through woods in the hour-before-dawn dark.
Evil air, a frost-making stillness,

Not a leaf, not a bird –
A world cast in frost. I came out above the wood

Where my breath left tortuous statues in the iron light.
But the valleys were draining the darkness

Till the moorline – blackening dregs of the
       brightening grey –
Halved the sky ahead. And I saw the horses:

Huge in the dense grey – ten together –
Megalith-still. They breathed, making no move,

With draped manes and tilted hind-hooves,
Making no sound.

I passed: not one snorted or jerked its head.
Grey silent fragments

Of a grey silent world.

I listened in emptiness on the moor-ridge.
The curlew's tear turned its edge on the silence.

Slowly detail leafed from the darkness. Then the sun
Orange, red, red erupted

164

Silently, and splitting to its core tore and flung cloud,
Shook the gulf open, showed blue,

And the big planets hanging –.
I turned

Stumbling in the fever of a dream, down towards
The dark woods, from the kindling tops,

And came to the horses.
                           There, still they stood,
But now steaming and glistening under the flow of light,

Their draped stone manes, their tilted hind-hooves
Stirring under a thaw while all around them

The frost showed its fires. But still they made no sound.
Not one snorted or stamped,

Their hung heads patient as the horizons,
High over valleys, in the red levelling rays –

In din of the crowded streets, going among the years,
        the faces,
May I still meet my memory in so lonely a place

Between the streams and the red clouds, hearing curlews,
Hearing the horizons endure.

TED HUGHES   165

HORSES, M62

Sprung from a field,
a team
of a dozen or so

is suddenly here and amongst,
silhouettes
in the butterscotch dusk.

One ghosts
between vans,
traverses three lanes,

its chess-piece head
fording the river of fumes;
one jumps the barricades

between carriageways;
a third slows
to a halt

then bends, nosing
the road, tonguing the surface
for salt.

Standstill.
Motor oil pulses.
Black blood.

Some trucker
swings down from his cab
to muster and drove; but

unbiddable, crossbred nags
they scatter
through ginnels

of coachwork and chrome,
and are distant, gone,
then a dunch

and here alongside
is a horse,
the writhing mat of its hide

pressed on the glass –
a tank of worms –
a flank

of actual horse . . .
It bolts,
all arse and tail

through a valley
of fleet saloons.
Regrouped they clatter away,

then spooked by a horn
double back,
a riderless charge,

a flack of horseshoe and hoof
into the idling cars,
now eyeball, nostril, tooth

under the sodium glow,
biblical, eastbound,
against the flow.

A BLESSING

Just off the highway to Rochester, Minnesota,
Twilight bounds softly forth on the grass.
And the eyes of those two Indian ponies
Darken with kindness.
They have come gladly out of the willows
To welcome my friend and me.
We step over the barbed wire into the pasture
Where they have been grazing all day, alone.
They ripple tensely, they can hardly contain their
    happiness
That we have come.
They bow shyly as wet swans. They love each other.
There is no loneliness like theirs.
At home once more,
They begin munching the young tufts of spring in the
    darkness.
I would like to hold the slenderer one in my arms,
For she has walked over to me
And nuzzled my left hand.
She is black and white,
Her mane falls wild on her forehead,
And the light breeze moves me to caress her long ear
That is delicate as the skin over a girl's wrist.
Suddenly I realize
That if I stepped out of my body I would break
Into blossom.

JAMES WRIGHT   169

HEAT

My mare, when she was in heat,
would travel the fenceline for hours,
wearing the impatience
in her feet into the ground.

Not a stallion for miles, I'd assure her,
give it up.

She'd widen her nostrils,
sieve the wind for news, be moving again,
her underbelly darkening with sweat,
then stop at the gate a moment, wait
to see what I might do.
Oh, I knew
how it was for her, easily
recognized myself in that wide lust:
came to stand in the pasture
just to see it played.
Offered a hand, a bucket of grain –
a minute's distraction from passion
the most I gave.

Then she'd return to what burned her:
the fence, the fence,
so hoping I might see, might let her free.

I'd envy her then,
to be so restlessly sure
of heat, and need, and what it takes
to feed the wanting that we are —

only a gap to open
the width of a mare,
the rest would take care of itself.
Surely, surely I knew that,
who had the power of bucket
and bridle —
she would beseech me, sidle up,
be gone, as life is short.
But desire, desire is long.

IN HIGH COUNTRY

It is easy to think you have done well,
Moving along in the beautiful. So much to praise
By the fire before sleep. Until a severed pine,

Absence. This is how you remember
Where you are: the marked tree, watershed
Understood by map, altitude traced

Ring by ring. While at your back the trail
Lapses, even as you keep the mountain
In sight. Branches close, flower after flower
Rise again to their places. In this country

Each step becomes an argument
For the last. Your horse will not climb
Until you do, and when it is time,
He will only head back by how he came.

TAKING LEAVE OF A FRIEND

Blue mountains to the north of the walls,
White river winding about them;
Here we must make separation
And go out through a thousand miles of dead grass,
Mind like a floating wide cloud,
Sunset like the parting of old acquaintances
Who bow over their clasped hands at a distance.
Our horses neigh to each other
　　　　　　as we are departing.

RIHAKU

TRANS. EZRA POUND

THE FACE OF THE HORSE

Animals do not sleep. At night
They stand over the world like a stone wall.

The cow's retreating head
Rustles the straw with its smooth horns,
The rocky brow a wedge
Between age-old cheek bones,
And the mute eyes
Turning sluggishly.

There's more intelligence and beauty in the
        horse's face.
He hears the talk of leaves and stones.
Intent, he knows the animal's cry
And the nightingale's murmur in the copse.

And knowing all, to whom may he recount
His wonderful visions?
The night is hushed. In the dark sky
Constellations rise.
The horse stands like a knight keeping watch,
The wind plays in his light hair,
His eyes burn like two huge worlds,
And his mane lifts like the imperial purple.

And if a man should see
The horse's magical face,
He would tear out his own impotent tongue
And give it to the horse. For
This magical creature is surely worthy of it.

Then we should hear words.
Words large as apples. Thick
As honey or buttermilk.
Words which penetrate like flame
And, once within the soul, like fire in some hut,
Illuminate its wretched trappings.
Words which do not die
And which we celebrate in song

But now the stable is empty,
The trees have dispersed,
Pinch-faced morning has swaddled the hills,
Unlocked the fields for work.
And the horse, caged within its shafts,
Dragging a covered wagon,
Gazes out of its meek eyes,
Upon the enigmatic, stationary world.

NIKOLAI ALEKSEEVICH ZABOLOTSKY   175
TRANS. DANIEL WEISSBORT

TWO HORSES PLAYING IN THE ORCHARD

Too soon, too soon, a man will come
To lock the gate, and drive them home.
Then, neighing softly through the night,
The mare will nurse her shoulder bite.
Now, lightly fair, through lock and mane
She gazes over the dusk again,
And sees her darkening stallion leap
In grass for apples, half asleep.

Lightly, lightly, on slender knees
He turns, lost in a dream of trees.
Apples are slow to find this day,
Someone has stolen the best away.
Still, some remain before the snow,
A few, trembling on boughs so low
A horse can reach them, small and sweet:
And some are tumbling to her feet.

Too soon, a man will scatter them,
Although I do not know his name,
His age, or how he came to own
A horse, an apple tree, a stone.
I let those horses in to steal
On principle, because I feel
Like half a horse myself, although
Too soon, too soon, already. Now.

BRONZES

The bronze General Grant riding a bronze horse in
    Lincoln Park
Shrivels in the sun by day when the motor cars whirr
    by in long processions going somewhere to keep
appointment for dinner and matinées and buying
    and selling
Though in the dusk and nightfall when high waves
    are piling
On the slabs of the promenade along the lake shore
    near by
  I have seen the general dare the combers come closer
And make to ride his bronze horse out into the hoofs
    and guns of the storm.

I cross Lincoln Park on a winter night when the snow
    is falling.
Lincoln in bronze stands among the white lines of
    snow, his bronze forehead meeting soft echoes
    of the newsies crying forty thousand men are
    dead along the Yser, his bronze ears listening to
    the mumbled roar of the city at his bronze feet.
A lithe Indian on a bronze pony, Shakespeare seated
    with long legs in bronze, Garibaldi in a bronze
    cape, they hold places in the cold, lonely snow
    to-night on their pedestals and so they will hold
    them past midnight and into the dawn.

A COUNTRY BOY IN WINTER

The wind may blow the snow about,
    For all I care, says Jack,
And I don't mind how cold it grows,
    For then the ice won't crack.
Old folks may shiver all day long,
    But I shall never freeze;
What cares a jolly boy like me
    For winter days like these?

Far down the long snow-covered hills
    It is such fun to coast,
So clear the road! the fastest sled
    There is in school I boast.
The paint is pretty well worn off,
    But then I take the lead;
A dandy sled's a loiterer,
    And I go in for speed.

When I go home at supper-time,
    Ki! but my cheeks are red!
They burn and sting like anything;
    I'm cross until I'm fed.
You ought to see the biscuit go,
    I am so hungry then;
And old Aunt Polly says that boys
    Eat twice as much as men.

There's always something I can do
    To pass the time away;
The dark comes quick in winter-time –
    A short and stormy day
And when I give my mind to it,
    It's just as father says,
I almost do a man's work now,
    And help him many ways.

I shall be glad when I grow up
    And get all through with school,
I'll show them by-and-by that I
    Was not meant for a fool.
I'll take the crops off this old farm,
    I'll do the best I can.
A jolly boy like me won't be
    A dolt when he's a man.

I like to hear the old horse neigh
    Just as I come in sight,
The oxen poke me with their horns
    To get their hay at night.
Somehow the creatures seem like friends,
    And like to see me come.
Some fellows talk about New York,
    But I shall stay at home.

SARAH ORNE JEWETT   179

KISSING A HORSE

Of the two spoiled, barn-sour geldings
we owned that year, it was Red –
skittish and prone to explode
even at fourteen years – who'd let me
hold to my face his own: the massive labyrinthine
caverns of the nostrils, the broad plain
up the head to the eyes. He'd let me stroke
his coarse chin whiskers and take
his soft meaty underlip
in my hands, press my man's carnivorous
kiss to his grass-nipping upper half of one, just
so that I could smell
the long way his breath had come from the rain
and the sun, the lungs and the heart,
from a world that meant no harm.

THE OCRACOKE PONIES

They make a dignity of loneliness.
They are more beautiful because
they don't belong.

No one saw the first ones
swim ashore centuries ago,
nudged by waves into the marsh grasses.

When you look into their faces, there is no trace
of the ship seized with terror, the crashing waves
and the horses' cries when thrown overboard.

Every afternoon you ride your bicycle to the pasture
to watch the twitch of their manes and ivory tails
unroll a carpet of silence, to see ponies lost in dream.

But it isn't dream, that place
your mind drifts to, that museum of memory
inventoried in opposition to the present.

You felt it once on a plane,
taking off from a city you didn't want to leave,
the stranded moment when the plane lifts into the clouds.

That's not dream, it's not even sleeping.
It is the nature of sleeping to be unaware.
This was some kind of waiting for the world to
        come back.

HORSES IN SNOW

They are a gift I have wanted again.
Wanted: One moment in mountains
when winter got so cold
the oil froze before it could burn.
I chopped ferns of hoarfrost from all the windows
and peered up at pines, a wedding cake
by a baker gone mad. Swirls by the thousand
shimmered above me until a cloud
lumbered over a ridge,
bringing the heavier white of more flurries.

I believed, I believed, I believed
it would last, that when you went out
to test the black ice or to dig out a Volkswagen
filled with rich women, you'd return
and we'd sputter like oil,
match after match, warm in the making.
Wisconsin's flat farmland never approved:
I hid in cornfields far into October,
listening to music that whirled from my thumbprint.
When sunset played havoc with bright leaves of alders,

I never mentioned longing or fear.
I crouched like a good refugee in brown creeks
and forgot why Autumn is harder than Spring.

But snug on the western slope of that mountain
I'd accept every terror, break open seals
to release love's headwaters to unhurried sunlight.
Weren't we Big Hearts? Through some trick of silver
we held one another, believing each motion the real one,
ah, lover, why were dark sources bundled up
in our eyes? Each owned an agate,

marbled with anguish, a heart or its echo,
we hardly knew. Lips touching lips,
did that break my horizon
as much as those horses broke my belief?
You drove off and I walked the old road,
scolding the doubles that wanted so much.
The chestnut mare whinnied a cloud into scrub pine.
In a windless corner of a corral,
four horses fit like puzzle pieces.
Their dark eyes and lashes defined by the white.

The colt kicked his hind, loped from the fence.
The mares and a stallion galloped behind,
lifting and leaping, finding each other
in full accord with the earth and their bodies.
No harm ever touched them once they cut loose,
snorting at flurries falling again.

How little our chances for feeling ourselves.
They vanished so quickly – one flick of a tail.
Where do their mountains and moments begin?
I stood a long time in sharpening wind.

LYING IN A HAMMOCK AT WILLIAM DUFFY'S FARM IN PINE ISLAND, MINNESOTA

Over my head, I see the bronze butterfly,
Asleep on the black trunk,
Blowing like a leaf in green shadow.
Down the ravine behind the empty house,
The cowbells follow one another
Into the distances of the afternoon.
To my right,
In a field of sunlight between two pines,
The droppings of last year's horses
Blaze up into golden stones.
I lean back, as the evening darkens and comes on.
A chicken hawk floats over, looking for home.
I have wasted my life.

THE HORSE'S MOUTH

They bought the horse
in Portobello
brought it home
could hardly wait
installed it in the living room
next to knitted dinner plate

Next to ashtray
(formerly bedpan)
euphonium
no one can play
camel-saddle dollypeg
wooden gollywog with tray

Near a neo
deco lampshade
(a snip at
thirty-seven quid)
castanets and hula-hoop
trunk with psychedelic lid

Under front end
of a caribou
next to foam-
filled rollerskate

(made by a girl in Camden Lock
– she of knitted dinner plate)

Uprooted from
its carousel
the painted horse
now laid to waste
amidst expensive bric-à-brac
and sterile secondhand bad taste

And each night as Mr and Ms Trend
in brassbed they lie dreaming
the horse in downstairs darkness
mouths a silent screaming.

ALL SUMMER LONG

The dogs eat hoof slivers and lie under the porch.
A strand of human hair hangs strangely from
    a fruit tree
like a cry in the throat. The sky is clay for the child
    who is past
being tired, who wanders in waist-deep
grasses. Gnats rise in a vapor,
in a long mounting whine around her forehead
    and ears.

The sun is an indistinct moon. Frail sticks
of grass poke her ankles,
and a wet froth of spiders touches her legs
like wet fingers. The musk and smell
of air are as hot as the savory
terrible exhales from a tired horse.

The parents are sleeping all afternoon,
and no one explains the long uneasy afternoons.
She hears their combined breathing and swallowing
salivas, and sees their sides rising and falling
like the sides of horses in the hot pasture.

At evening a breeze dries and crumbles
the sky and the clouds float like undershirts
and cotton dresses on a clothesline. Horses
rock to their feet and race or graze.
Parents open their shutters and call
the lonely, happy child home.
The child who hates silences talks and talks
of cicadas and the manes of horses.

ALL THE LITTLE HOOF-PRINTS

Farther up the gorge the sea's voice fainted and ceased.
We heard a new noise far away ahead of us, vague and
metallic, it might have been some unpleasant
bird's voice
Bedded in a matrix of long silences. At length we came
to a little cabin lost in the redwoods,
An old man sat on a bench before the doorway filing a
cross-cut saw; sometimes he slept,
Sometimes he filed. Two or three horses in the corral
by the streamside lifted their heads
To watch us pass, but the old man did not.

       In the afternoon we returned the same way,
And had the picture in our minds of magnificent
regions of space and mountain not seen before.
(This was
The first time that we visited Pigeon Gap, whence you
look down behind the great shouldering pyramid-
Edges of Pico Blanco through eagle-gulfs of air to a
forest basin
Where two-hundred-foot redwoods look like the pile on
a Turkish carpet.) With such extensions of the idol-
Worshipping mind we came down the streamside. The
old man was still at his post by the cabin doorway,
but now

Stood up and stared, said angrily 'Where are you
    camping?' I said 'We're not camping, we're going
    home.' He said
From his flushed heavy face, 'That's the way fires get
    started. Did you come at night?' 'We passed you
    this morning.
You were half asleep, filing a saw.' 'I'll kill anybody
    that starts a fire here...' his voice quavered
Into bewilderment... 'I didn't see you. Kind of feeble
    I guess.
My temperature's a hundred and two every afternoon.'
    'Why, what's the matter?' He removed his hat
And rather proudly showed us a deep healed trench in
    the bald skull. 'My horse fell at the ford,
I must 'a' cracked my head on a rock. Well sir I can't
    remember anything till next morning.
I woke in bed the pillow was soaked with blood, the
    horse was in the corral and had had his hay,' –
Singing the words as if he had told the story a hundred
    times. To whom? To himself, probably, –
'The saddle was on the rack and the bridle on the right
    nail. What do you think of *that* now?' He passed
His hand on his bewildered forehead and said, 'Unless
    an angel or something came down and did it.
A basin of blood and water by the crick, I must 'a'

washed myself.' My wife said sharply, 'Have you
     been to a doctor?'
'Oh yes,' he said, 'my boy happened down.' She said 'You
     oughtn't to be alone here: are you all alone here?'
'No;' he answered, 'horses. I've been all over the world:
     right here is the most beautiful place in the world.
I played the piccolo in ships' orchestras.' We looked at
     the immense redwoods and dark
Fern-taken slip of land by the creek, where the horses
     were, and the yuccaed hillsides high in the sun
Flaring like torches; I said 'Darkness comes early here.'
     He answered with pride and joy, 'Two hundred and
     eighty-
Five days in the year the sun never gets in here.
Like living under the sea, green all summer, beautiful.'
     My wife said, 'How do you know your temperature's
A hundred and two?' 'Eh? The doctor. He said the bone
Presses my brain, he's got to cut out a piece. I said All
     right you've got to wait till it rains,
I've got to guard my place through the fire-season.
     By God' he said joyously,
'The quail on my roof wake me up every morning, then
     I look out the window and a dozen deer
Drift up the canyon with the mist on their shoulders.
     Look in the dust at your feet, all the little
     hoof-prints.'

THE HORSE

The horse moves
independently
without reference
to his load

He has eyes
like a woman and
turns them
about, throws

back his ears
and is generally
conscious of
the world. Yet

he pulls when
he must and
pulls well, blowing
fog from

his nostrils
like fumes from
the twin
exhausts of a car.

WILLIAM CARLOS WILLIAMS

THE LISTENERS

'Is there anybody there?' said the Traveller,
    Knocking on the moonlit door;
And his horse in the silence champed the grasses
    Of the forest's ferny floor:
And a bird flew up out of the turret,
    Above the Traveller's head:
And he smote upon the door again a second time;
    'Is there anybody there?' he said.
But no one descended to the Traveller;
    No head from the leaf-fringed sill
Leaned over and looked into his grey eyes,
    Where he stood perplexed and still.
But only a host of phantom listeners
    That dwelt in the lone house then
Stood listening in the quiet of the moonlight
    To that voice from the world of men:
Stood thronging the faint moonbeams on the dark stair,
    That goes down to the empty hall,
Hearkening in an air stirred and shaken
    By the lonely Traveller's call.
And he felt in his heart their strangeness,
    Their stillness answering his cry,
While his horse moved, cropping the dark turf,
    'Neath the starred and leafy sky;

For he suddenly smote on the door, even
   Louder, and lifted his head: –
'Tell them I came, and no one answered,
   That I kept my word,' he said.
Never the least stir made the listeners,
   Though every word he spake
Fell echoing through the shadowiness of the still house
   From the one man left awake:
Ay, they heard his foot upon the stirrup,
   And the sound of iron on stone,
And how the silence surged softly backward,
   When the plunging hoofs were gone.

NO BUYERS

A Load of brushes and baskets and cradles and chairs
 Labours along the street in the rain:
With it a man, a woman, a pony with whiteybrown
  hairs. –
 The man foots in front of the horse with a shambling
  sway
  At a slower tread than a funeral train,
 While to a dirge-like tune he chants his wares,
Swinging a Turk's-head brush (in a drum-major's way
   When the bandsmen march and play).

A yard from the back of the man is the whiteybrown
  pony's nose:
He mirrors his master in every item of pace and pose:
 He stops when the man stops, without being told,
 And seems to be eased by a pause; too plainly he's old,
  Indeed, not strength enough shows
 To steer the disjointed waggon straight,
 Which wriggles left and right in a rambling line,
 Deflected thus by its own warp and weight,
 And pushing the pony with it in each incline.

 The woman walks on the pavement verge,
  Parallel to the man:
She wears an apron white and wide in span,

And carries a like Turk's-head, but more in nursing-wise:
    Now and then she joins in his dirge,
    But as if her thoughts were on distant things,
    The rain clams her apron till it clings. –
So, step by step, they move with their merchandise,
      And nobody buys.

THE KING'S HORSES

After fifty years, nearly, I remember,
living then in a quiet leafy suburb,
waking in the darkness, made aware
of a continuous irregular noise,
and groping to the side window to discover
the shadow-shapes which made that muffled patter
passing across the end of our avenue,
the black trees and the streetlights shuttering
a straggle of flowing shadows, endless, of horses.

Gypsies they could have been, or tinkers maybe,
mustering to some hosting of their clans,
or horse-dealers heading their charges to the docks,
timed to miss the day's traffic and alarms:
a migration the newspapers had not foretold;
some battle's ragged finish, dream repeated:
the last of an age retreating, withdrawing,
leaving us beggared, bereft
of the proud nodding muzzles, the nervous bodies:
gone from us the dark men with their ancient skills
of saddle and stirrup, or bridle and breeding.

It was an end, I was sure, but an end of what
I never could tell. It was never reported:
But the echoing hooves persisted. Years after,

In a London hotel in the grey dawn
A serious man concerned with certain duties,
I heard again the metal clatter of hooves staccato
And hurriedly rose to catch a glimpse of my horses,
But the pace and beat were utterly different:
I saw by the men astride these were the King's horses
Going about the King's business, never mine.

'WHEN IN YOUR *NEIGHBORHOOD* YOU HEAR A *NEIGH*'

When in your *neighborhood* you hear a *neigh*,
It means that there's a horse not far away.

CELEBRATION AND
REMEMBRANCE

THE OLD WHIM HORSE

He's an old grey horse, with his head bowed sadly,
    And with dim old eyes and a queer roll aft,
With the off-fore sprung and the hind screwed badly,
    And he bears all over the brands of graft;
And he lifts his head from the grass to wonder
    Why by night and day the whim is still,
Why the silence is, and the stampers' thunder
    Sounds forth no more from the shattered mill.

In that whim he worked when the night winds bellowed
    On the riven summit of Giant's Hand,
And by day when prodigal Spring had yellowed
    All the wide, long sweep of enchanted land;
And he knew his shift, and the whistle's warning,
    And he knew the calls of the boys below;
Through the years, unbidden, at night or morning,
    He had taken his stand by the old whim bow.

But the whim stands still, and the wheeling swallow
    In the silent shaft hangs her home of clay,
And the lizards flirt and the swift snakes follow
    O'er the grass-grown brace in the summer day;
And the corn springs high in the cracks and corners
    Of the forge, and down where the timber lies;
And the crows are perched like a band of mourners
    On the broken hut on the Hermit's Rise.

All the hands have gone, for the rich reef paid out,
    And the company waits till the calls come in;
But the old grey horse, like the claim, is played out,
    And no market's near for his bones and skin.
So they let him live, and they left him grazing
    By the creek, and oft in the evening dim
I have seen him stand on the rises, gazing
    At the ruined brace and the rotting whim.

The floods rush high in the gully under,
    And the lightnings lash at the shrinking trees,
Or the cattle down from the ranges blunder
    As the fires drive by on the summer breeze.
Still the feeble horse at the right hour wanders
    To the lonely ring, though the whistle's dumb,
And with hanging head by the bow he ponders
    Where the whim boy's gone – why the shifts
        don't come.

But there comes a night when he sees lights glowing
    In the roofless huts and the ravaged mill,
When he hears again all the stampers going –
    Though the huts are dark and the stampers still:
When he sees the steam to the black roof clinging
    As its shadows roll on the silver sands,
And he knows the voice of his driver singing,
    And the knocker's clang where the braceman stands.

See the old horse take, like a creature dreaming,
    On the ring once more his accustomed place;
But the moonbeams full on the ruins streaming
    Show the scattered timbers and grass-grown brace.
Yet HE hears the sled in the smithy falling,
    And the empty truck as it rattles back,
And the boy who stands by the anvil, calling;
    And he turns and backs, and he 'takes up slack'.

While the old drum creaks, and the shadows shiver
    As the wind sweeps by, and the hut doors close,
And the bats dip down in the shaft or quiver
    In the ghostly light, round the grey horse goes;
And he feels the strain on his untouched shoulder,
    Hears again the voice that was dear to him,
Sees the form he knew – and his heart grows bolder
    As he works his shift by the broken whim.

He hears in the sluices the water rushing
    As the buckets drain and the doors fall back;
When the early dawn in the east is blushing,
    He is limping still round the old, old track.
Now he pricks his ears, with a neigh replying
    To a call unspoken, with eyes aglow,
And he sways and sinks in the circle, dying;
    From the ring no more will the grey horse go.

In a gully green, where a dam lies gleaming,
   And the bush creeps back on a worked-out claim,
And the sleepy crows in the sun sit dreaming
   On the timbers grey and a charred hut frame,
Where the legs slant down, and the hare is squatting
   In the high rank grass by the dried-up course,
Nigh a shattered drum and a king-post rotting
   Are the bleaching bones of the old grey horse.

POOR OLD DEAD HORSES

Don't give your rocking-horse
To the old rag and bony

He'll go straight to the knacker
And haggle for money

The stirrups are torn off
The bridle and harness

Chopped up for firewood
It is thrown on the furnace

And the water that boils
Is chucked down the sluices

To wash away what remains
Of poor old dead horses.

ROGER McGOUGH

THE HOSS

'The hoss he is a splendud beast;
He is man's friend, as heaven desined,
And, search the world from west to east,
No honester you'll ever find!

'Some calls the hoss "a pore dumb brute,"
And yit, like Him who died fer you,
I say, as I theyr charge refute,
"Fergive; they know not what they do!"

'No wiser animal makes tracks
Upon these earthly shores, and hence
Arose the axium, true as facts,
Extoled by all, as "Good hoss-sense!"

'The hoss is strong, and knows his stren'th, –
You hitch him up a time er two
And lash him, and he'll go his len'th
And kick the dashboard out fer you!

'But, treat him allus good and kind,
And never strike him with a stick,
Ner aggervate him, and you'll find
He'll never do a hostile trick.

'A hoss whose master tends him right
And worters him with daily care,
Will do your biddin' with delight,
And act as docile as YOU air.

'He'll paw and prance to hear your praise,
Because he's learnt to love you well;
And, though you can't tell what he says
He'll nicker all he wants to tell.

'He knows you when you slam the gate
At early dawn, upon your way
Unto the barn, and snorts elate,
To git his corn, er oats, er hay.

'He knows you, as the orphant knows
The folks that loves her like theyr own,
And raises her and "finds" her clothes,
And "schools" her tel a womern-grown!

'I claim no hoss will harm a man,
Ner kick, ner run away, cavort,
Stump-suck, er balk, er "catamaran,"
Ef you'll jest treat him as you ort.

209

'But when I see the beast abused,
And clubbed around as I've saw some,
I want to see his owner noosed,
And jest yanked up like Absolum!

'Of course they's differunce in stock, –
A hoss that has a little yeer,
And slender build, and shaller hock,
Can beat his shadder, mighty near!

'Whilse one that's thick in neck and chist
And big in leg and full in flank,
That tries to race, I still insist
He'll have to take the second rank.

'And I have jest laid back and laughed,
And rolled and wallered in the grass
At fairs, to see some heavy-draft
Lead out at FIRST, yit come in LAST!

'Each hoss has his appinted place, –
The heavy hoss should plow the soil; –
The blooded racer, he must race,
And win big wages fer his toil.

'I never bet – ner never wrought
Upon my feller man to bet –
And yit, at times, I've often thought
Of my convictions with regret.

'I bless the hoss from hoof to head –
From head to hoof, and tale to mane! –
I bless the hoss, as I have said,
From head to hoof, and back again!

'I love my God the first of all,
Then Him that perished on the cross,
And next, my wife, – and then I fall
Down on my knees and love the hoss.'

JAMES WHITCOMB RILEY

WINNIE

When I went by the meadow gate
The chestnut mare would trot to meet me,
And as her coming I would wait,
She'd whinny high as if to greet me.
And I would kiss her silky nose,
And stroke her neck until it glistened,
And speak soft words: I don't suppose
She understand – but how she listened!

Then in the war-net I was caught,
Returning three black winters older;
And when the little mare I sought
The farmer told me he had sold her.
And so time passed – when in the street
One day I heard a plaintive whinny
That roused a recollection sweet,
So then I turned and there was Winnie.

I vow she knew me, mooning there.
She raised her nose for me to fondle,
And though I'd lost an arm I'll swear
She kissed the empty sleeve a-dangle.
But oh it cut me to the heart,
Though I was awful glad to meet her,
For lo! she dragged a tinker's cart
And stumbled weakly as he beat her.

Just skin and bone, a sorry hack!
Say, fellow, you may think it funny:
I made a deal and bought her back,
Though it took all my bonus money.
And she'll be in the meadow there,
As long as I have dough for spending...
Gee! I'll take care of that old mare –
'Sweetheart! you'll have a happy ending.'

THE AULD FARMER'S NEW-YEAR-MORNING SALUTATION TO HIS AULD MARE, MAGGIE

A Guide New-year I wish thee, Maggie!
Hae, there's a ripp to thy auld baggie:
Tho' thou's howe-backit now, an' knaggie,
I've seen the day
There could hae gaen like ony staggie,
Out-owre the lay.

Tho' now thou's dowie, stiff an' crazy,
An' thy auld hide as white's a daisie,
I've seen the dappl't, sleek an' glaizie,
A bonie gray:
He should been tight that daur't to raize thee,
Ance in a day.

Thou ance was i' the foremost rank,
A filly buirdly, steeve an' swank;
An' set weel down a shapely shank,
As e'er tread yird;
An' could hae flown out-owre a stank,
Like ony bird.

It's now some nine-an'-twenty year,
Sin' thou was my guid-father's mear;
He gied me thee, o' tocher clear,
An' fifty mark;
Tho' it was sma', 'twas weel-won gear,
An' thou was stark.

When first I gaed to woo my Jenny,
Ye then was trotting wi' your minnie:
Tho' ye was trickie, slee, an funnie,
Ye ne'er was donsie;
But hamely, tawie, quiet, an' cannie,
An' unco sonsie.

That day, ye pranc'd wi' muckle pride,
When ye bure hame my bonie bride:
An' sweet an' gracefu' she did ride,
Wi' maiden air!
Kyle-Stewart I could bragged wide
For sic a pair.

Tho' now ye dow but hoyte and hobble,
An' wintle like a saumont coble,
That day, ye was a jinker noble,
For heels an' win'!
An' ran them till they a' did wauble,
Far, far, behin'!

When thou an' I were young an' skeigh
An' stable-meals at fairs were dreigh,
How thou wad prance, and snore, an' skreigh
An' tak the road!
Town's-bodies ran, an' stood abeigh,
An' ca't thee mad.

When thou was corn't, an' I was mellow,
We took the road aye like a swallow:
At brooses thou had ne'er a fellow,
For pith an' speed;
But ev'ry tail thou pay't them hollow,
Whare'er thou gaed.

The sma', droop-rumpl't, hunter cattle
Might aiblins waurt thee for a brattle;
But sax Scotch mile, thou try't their mettle,
An' gar't them whaizle:
Nae whip nor spur, but just a wattle
O' saugh or hazel.

Thou was a noble fittie-lan',
As e'er in tug or tow was drawn!
Aft thee an' I, in aught hours' gaun,
In guid March-weather,
Hae turn'd sax rood beside our han',
For days thegither.

Thou never braing't, an' fetch't, an' fliskit;
But thy auld tail thou wad hae whiskit,
An' spread abreed thy weel-fill'd brisket,
Wi' pith an' power;
Till sprittie knowes wad rair't an' riskit
An' slypet owre.

When frosts lay lang, an' snaws were deep,
An' threaten'd labour back to keep,
I gied thy cog a wee bit heap
Aboon the timmer:
I ken'd my Maggie wad na sleep,
For that, or simmer.

In cart or car thou never reestit;
The steyest brae thou wad hae fac't it;
Thou never lap, an' sten't, and breastit,
Then stood to blaw;
But just thy step a wee thing hastit,
Thou snoov't awa.

My pleugh is now thy bairn-time a',
Four gallant brutes as e'er did draw;
Forbye sax mae I've sell't awa,
That thou hast nurst:
They drew me thretteen pund an' twa,
The vera warst.

Mony a sair daurk we twa hae wrought,
An' wi' the weary warl' fought!
An' mony an anxious day, I thought
We wad be beat!
Yet here to crazy age we're brought,
Wi' something yet.

An' think na', my auld trusty servan',
That now perhaps thou's less deservin,
An' thy auld days may end in starvin;
For my last fow,
A heapit stimpart, I'll reserve ane
Laid by for you.

We've worn to crazy years thegither;
We'll toyte about wi' ane anither;
Wi' tentie care I'll flit thy tether
To some hain'd rig,
Whare ye may nobly rax your leather,
Wi' sma' fatigue.

A MARE

Lovely Fia was the summer queen
And the sun-bodied light of winter: she so slender
Of pastern, fine of cannon, sloped in the shoulders
To all perfection, with that gazelle head set
Arched beneath the drawn bow of her neck;
She who rose blazing from the dusky stall
And lunged on the snaffle, who reared on high white
    stockings,
Light-mouthed, light-footed, blasting her loud whinny,
Saying among the oak trees, 'Ha ha!' She was a mirror
Of flame, and when she ran, then she ran burning,
Swift as the falcon that stoops through the windless sky.

Fiamma, who can tell of all your richness?
You were a dragon horde, gold-red and willful.
How dark the winter rains are falling now!
I cannot find your peer in any pasture.

THE HORSE

For Ichiro Kawamoto, humanitarian,
electrician, & survivor of Hiroshima

They spoke of the horse alive
without skin, naked, hairless,
without eyes and ears, searching
for the stable boy's caress.
Shoot it, someone said, but they
let him go on colliding with
tattered walls, butting his long
skull to pulp, finding no path
where iron fences corkscrewed in
the street and bicycles turned
like question marks.
                    Some fled and
some sat down. The river burned
all that day and into the
night, the stones sighed a moment
and were still, and the shadow
of a man's hand entered
a leaf.

The white horse never
returned, and later they found
the stable boy, his back crushed
by a hoof, his mouth opened
around a cry that no one heard.

They spoke of the horse again
and again; their mouths opened
like the gills of a fish caught
above water.
            Mountain flowers
burst from the red clay walls, and
they said a new life was here.
Raw grass sprouted from the cobbles
like hair from a deafened ear.
The horse would never return.

There had been no horse. I could
tell from the way they walked
testing the ground for some cold
that the rage had gone out of
their bones in one mad dance.

WHEN IT WAS TIME

He did not carry the body up, he could not,
After all it was a horse and so instead
He asked the horse to carry him

As far as possible, while the animal believed
They were on some mission, like searching
For poachers up on the ridge, or other signs

Of trespass, and with great difficulty
Breathed, climbed and kept turning
To see what the man was doing;

The horse that believed something ordinary
Was about to happen and the man who believed
He was moving into what he must now do

But suddenly found himself unable,
Having come to the place
Of one time too many, the terrain worn down

By many years of this, this love of another
Who will move, carry, or even bend when and
        wherever the man wishes.
He propped the gun up against the tree

As he sat in the dirt and the dark came on,
And the horse who watched was becoming changed
And later would go away knowing nothing ever
     bound him

To the rock up there, where what the man would do
And what he would not do still unravels.

A TWENTY-FOURTH POEM
ABOUT HORSES

Night deepening, frost leans on the stables
of thoroughbreds, west wind splitting their hooves.
– LI HO, 'Twenty-Three Poems About Horses'

Steed out of my dusk and a dusk, now, for the species,
veins deltawise down your silky inner thigh,

veins trickling from one eye down the roan cliffside
of a nose vaulted and chanceled for winds of the
      Pleistocene,

you have come, you paw patiently, that is the main thing,
the fields between stretch wider and we, the restless,
      are everywhere

save where your nostril quivers, arches, and you snort
      in the night.
We who debouch into all places dream of you now
      nowhere.

You come to a woman's hand: that smile. You come to a
child's hand, giggling and shivers. Your hot breath
      pleasures soldiers.

Harnessed to caisson with bannered coffin, to the
    barouche
at a state wedding, you are ambassador from the eldest
    kingdom.

The King of Brazil sent a forest of teak to pave the
    streets
girdling the Pantheon, to muffle the clatter you hauled
    there.

When we spurred you against Wellington's infantry
    squares,
you side ran them or reared back. The god of
    catastrophes took note.

Sad banner you were in the prophecies of Sweet
    Medicine,
the whiskered whitneys bringing and spawning your
    manes and tails

among the Arapaho, Cheyenne, Lakota, Kiowa,
your speed between their loins a drumming
        into decline.

Under Tutankhamun, the generalissimo who rode you
    hummed
his tenth title: Overseer of Works in the Hill of
    Gritstone,

Muir knew you on both shores, and van der Post
    knew you,
mufti lords recognizing a lord in service. Nuzzle
    them both.

They say that Poseidon at Onchestos, breaking you as
    a colt,
had your driver leap off where the road entered forest,

and watched to see what you'd do, the rig rattling –
    smash it
against the trunks on the run, or walk it through tall
    shadows.

Where you linger for shade on the veldt, branches
    level,
a tree is the only tree. Your water, the only water.

Flickers of hair along your neck's crest release
the only signal. Which staggers from storm cloud to
    browse oats.

Stubby melted candle, your recessed phallus makes
no howitzer but glistens a coat whose sheen ripples off.

For I imagine that Li Ho, seeing good men misused
as you were, foresaw your withdrawal from our night
        grasses.

For your standing here re-ordains neither Akhilleus
nor Cuchulain. Dew braids your mane with fresh
        constellations.

For what shall we make of you, made into goddess, mare
sacrificed but receiving cult also among the footloose

on the steppes: mother ridden by god-spear, great
        mam thus
captured, cinched, spurred? though your flanks shudder
        unfettered.

Through mists we flash bits of mirror, but from them
you pound abreast, neither parent, eyes orbing the
        two sides.

For that demigod's eye, tiding, capsizes anyone
who would turn trainer. And this one goes on into
        the bond.

A trainer aims at one thing, but what tingles him is force
hinting at the uncontainable, the opponent.

And the top tamers, spook-soothers, the whisperers,
will write their books but miss the appointment.
        It is not inscribed.

The two grooms beside you in Hokusai's whitewater
        cascade
lave you with splashes of it, currying your bulk,

hoisting your nosebag – and no one has set the timer,
        everywhere
it is one sound, stampede steadied and rocking in it.

Your great-grandparents, unicorn wild asses
from Persia and Scythia, fostered childbirth but also
        pissed plagues,

the unharnessable *summum totium* browsing in ocean,
an eye-spangled three-legged mountain. Hell and
        cloud in your seed!

It was your miniature stature at the beginning, Maria
        Tallchief
at ten, that wedged you between giants into the
        straightaway.

228

And the reindeer modeled from smudge in the Font de
      Gaume grotto
at Les Eyzies, fading across your body, trails a third
      antler

like a skater's scarf through your head, broadening out,
a dancer's arm rippling after the total gather.

Looking back from the pass at his mounted escorts,
      flashing them
three turns back down the corkscrew, the Fourteenth
      Dalai Lama

saw them slumped on your back, the red of Rahu in
      splashes
and trickling stillness. And dripping you still awaited
      their nudges.

In that patience, the kernel of the twister moan-lifting
over Kansas, the shrapnel clatter of your take-off.

Across that aftermath, bubbling through wind-sound
      or the mind's
rise from its cringe, the flubber-flutter of moody-
      moodlessness.

So the unforeseen from you opposes the blindly seen
in us —
your fuse as a spurter, jump-taker, yet a curb also

to our unsnaffled berserkness. For the berserking
Greek says
that only that ass's horn or hoof, cut off and cupped
upward,

can hold any of the cold torrent under the world,
implacable Styx. All else, graces or muons, it crumbles.

And every jot which that flow dissolves, the images
with their assessors, has rolled in us. And you have
stood

calmly beside us, your shot breath a bloom in the cold,
your hooves hammers yet also the last and only chalice.

The unreached-for cup, beaker for world-toxin,
breast englobing ground zero. And so we know
you not.

And I realize: though I have walked drenched in
spring rains
my bare thighs have not hugged your warm bellows in
a downpour.

230

For though your manic tribe is mine, the boreal
    chargers,
mere rooms, a migrant's mangy stations, have
    detained me.

For while historians of cultures hot on the spoor of
    roots among
their root clans have heard you drum past, they looked
    up only briefly.

For though engravers assumed you would stay, given
    their way with your
musculature, accoutrements, wavy harness, tip-toe
    grooms,

gear draped over your cruppers like an evening gown,
    its ratios
and metalwork continuous with Genghis Khan's and
    a jockey's,

their inky mastery frames cozily misleading questions:
which posthouse this evening, what pasture tomorrow?

Whereas you inquire into rupture and the unfenced:
    what thunder
between flesh and ground, what surge from the cells
    even past sundown?

JOHN PECK   231

DANSE MACABRE

The broken oarshaft was stuck in the hill
In the middle of chicory,
Puke-flowers, the farmers called them, sturdy
Little evangels that the white deer drift through ...

Nobody on the hill before
Had heard of a horse
Breaking its leg in a rowboat. But the mare
Leapt the fence, passed
The tar-paper henhouse,
And then crumpled at the shore.

It was April and bees were floating
In the cold evening barn; from the loft
We heard them shoot the poor horse.
We tasted gunpowder and looked
While your cousin, the sick
Little bastard, giggled and got
So excited he started to dance
Like the slow sweeping passes
Of a drawing compass –

Its cruel nail to its true pencil.

SEEING THE BONES

This year again the bruise-colored oak
hangs on eating my heart out
with its slow change, the leaves at last
spiraling end over end like your
letters home that fall Fridays
in the box at the foot of the hill
saying the old news, keeping it neutral.
You ask about the dog, fourteen years
your hero, deaf now as a turnip,
thin as kindling.

In junior high your biology class
boiled a chicken down into its bones
four days at a simmer in my pot,
then wired joint by joint
the re-created hen
in an anatomy project
you stayed home from, sick.

Thus am I afflicted, seeing the bones.
How many seasons walking
on fallen apples like pebbles in
the shoes of the Canterbury faithful
have I kept the garden up
with leaven of wood ash, kitchen leavings
and the sure reciprocation of horse dung?

How many seasons have the foals
come right or breeched or in good time
turned yearlings, two-year-olds, and at three
clattered off in a ferment to the sales?
Your ponies, those dapple-gray kings
of the orchard, long gone to skeleton,
gallop across the landscape of my dreams.
I meet my father there, dead years before
you left us for a European career.
He is looping the loop on a roller coaster
called Mercy, he is calling his children in.

I do the same things day by day.
They steady me against the wrong turn,
the closed-ward babel of anomie.

This Friday your letter in thinnest blue
script alarms me. Weekly you grow
more British with your *I shalls*
and now you're off to Africa
or Everest, daughter of the file drawer,
citizen of no return. I give
your britches, long outgrown, to the crows,
your boots with a summer visit's worth
of mud caked on them to the shrews
for nests if they will have them.

Working backward I reconstruct
you. Send me your baby teeth, some new
nail parings and a hank of hair
and let me do the rest. I'll
set the pot to boil.

THE HORSES

Barely a twelvemonth after
The seven days war that put the world to sleep,
Late in the evening the strange horses came.
By then we had made our covenant with silence,
But in the first few days it was so still
We listened to our breathing and were afraid.
On the second day
The radios failed; we turned the knobs; no answer.
On the third day a warship passed us, heading north,
Dead bodies piled on the deck. On the sixth day
A plane plunged over us into the sea. Thereafter
Nothing. The radios dumb;
And still they stand in corners of our kitchens,
And stand, perhaps, turned on, in a million rooms
All over the world. But now if they should speak,
If on a sudden they should speak again,
If on the stroke of noon a voice should speak,
We would not listen, we would not let it bring
That old bad world that swallowed its children quick
At one great gulp. We would not have it again.
Sometimes we think of the nations lying asleep,
Curled blindly in impenetrable sorrow,
And then the thought confounds us with its
        strangeness.
The tractors lie about our fields; at evening

They look like dank sea-monsters couched
        and waiting
We leave them where they are and let them rust:
"They'll moulder away and be like other loam'.
We make our oxen drag our rusty ploughs,
Long laid aside. We have gone back
Far past our fathers' land.
                                And then, that evening
Late in the summer the strange horses came.
We heard a distant tapping on the road,
A deepening drumming; it stopped, went on again
And at the corner changed to hollow thunder.
We saw the heads
Like a wild wave charging and were afraid.
We had sold our horses in our fathers' time
To buy new tractors. Now they were strange to us
As fabulous steeds set on an ancient shield
Or illustrations in a book of knights.
We did not dare go near them. Yet they waited,
Stubborn and shy, as if they had been sent
By an old command to find our whereabouts
And that long-lost archaic companionship.
In the first moment we had never a thought
That they were creatures to be owned and used.
Among them were some half a dozen colts

Dropped in some wilderness of the broken world,
Yet new as if they had come from their own Eden.
Since then they have pulled our ploughs and
    borne our load,
But that free servitude still can pierce our hearts.
Our life is changed; their coming our beginning.

INDEX OF AUTHORS

239

ACKNOWLEDGMENTS

Thanks are due to the following copyright holders for permission to reprint:

SIMON ARMITAGE: 'Horses, M62' from *Tyrannosaurus Rex Versus the Corduroy Kid* by Simon Armitage, copyright © 2006 by Simon Armitage. Used by permission of Alfred A. Knopf, a division of Random House, Inc. 'Horses, M62' from *Tyrannosaurus Rex Versus the Corduroy Kid* by Simon Armitage. Used by permission of Faber & Faber Limited. KATE BARNES: 'A Mare' by Kate Barnes, first published in *The New Yorker*. ROBIN BECKER: Sections 1, 2, 5, and 8 of the poem entitled 'The Horse Fair' taken from the book *The Horse Fair: Poems* by Robin Becker, © 2000. Reprinted by permission of the University of Pittsburgh Press. SOPHIE CABOT BLACK: 'Pulling Into Morning', 'In High Country' and 'When It Was Time' by Sophie Cabot Black. Copyright © Sophie Cabot Black. Reprinted from *The Descent* with the permission of Graywolf Press, Saint Paul, Minnesota and by kind permission of the poet. EAVAN BOLAND: 'The War Horse' from *An Origin Like Water: Collected Poems 1967–1987* by Eavan Boland. Copyright © 1996 by Eavan Boland. Used by permission of W. W. Norton & Company, Inc. 'The War Horse' from *An Origin Like Water: Collected Poems 1967–1987* by Eavan Boland. Used by permission of Carcanet Press Limited. JASON BREDLE: 'The Horse's Adventure' by Jason Bredle,

256